John Markey's brilliant reflection, *Moses* ⟨...⟩ enormous contribution to the existing literature on the preferential option for the poor and reminds us of the universal call to liberation. . . . Markey identifies the walls that confine the human spirit and breaks down the dualisms between "us" and "them." . . . As he reminds us that we cannot understand the mystery of our lives independently of the mystery of God, he also helps us see that we cannot understand who we are independently of our connection to one another, especially our neighbor in need.

—Daniel G. Groody, CSC
University of Notre Dame

[In *Moses in Pharaoh's House*, John Markey] has created a work of compelling power and intellectual depth that asks us to experience the world in a radically different way. If we are to imitate Christ, then we . . . must make choices in keeping with God's love for those at the economic and political margins of our world. Only then do we begin a dismantling of the walls of Pharaoh's house.

—Nancy Pineda-Madrid
Associate professor of theology, Boston College

In *Moses in Pharaoh's House*, John Markey provides us a deft pathway out of Pharaoh's house—moving toward a more authentic and engaged spirituality . . . that addresses both the oppressive elements of our culture and the consequences those elements have for other people around the world. . . . A must-read for those who seek liberation from what ails us and who want to create greater global solidarity.

—Robert Schreiter
Catholic Theological Union

Author Acknowledgments

This project began and emerged through the generosity and hospitality of Steve Bevans, Gary Riebe-Estrella, and Robert Schreiter. Their insights, feedback, and suggestions are present in every chapter of this book.

As this book developed into its current form, I was given help and encouragement from my colleagues and students at Oblate School of Theology in San Antonio, Texas. In particular, Ron Rolheiser and Scott Woodward believed in my work and aided my efforts. I am particularly grateful to Greg Zuschlag for his many suggestions, clarifications, and fresh perspectives.

Many people who contributed to the writing and rewriting of this text over the last two years may never fully know the depth of my appreciation. Among them are Bob Streit, Tony Streit, Esther Hurh, Lynn Streit, Cyd Crouse, Niels Caminada, Lloyd von Blyvelt, Kevin Tuerff, Rose Chalifoux, Gerry and Aimee Doran, and Paul Vance. I also give special thanks to Albert and Barbara Gelpi for their support, trust, and love over these many years.

My family is the source of my vocation as a theologian and my abiding belief in the possibilities of human growth and sanctification. In this regard, I am particularly appreciative of the love and example that my parents, Joe and Sharron Markey, have always provided me. During the process of creating this book, my brothers and sisters and their spouses and children have been sources of insight and inspiration. I also thank the brothers of the San Juan Macias Dominican Priory for their fraternal support over the past four years.

Finally, I am grateful for the help of Anthony Chiffolo, Paul Peterson, and Maura Thompson Hagarty for their hard work and genuine desire to bring this text to completion and nurture it into its final form.

Publisher Acknowledgments

Thank you to the following individuals who reviewed this work in progress:

Peter H. Beisheim, *Stonehill College, Easton, Massachusetts*

Patrick Lynch, *Canisius College, Buffalo, New York*

Joy Milos, *Gonzaga University, Spokane, Washington*

Eilish Ryan, *University of the Incarnate Word, San Antonio, Texas*

Richard C. Salter, *Hobart and William Smith Colleges, Geneva, New York*

MOSES
IN PHARAOH'S
HOUSE

A LIBERATION SPIRITUALITY FOR NORTH AMERICA

JOHN J. MARKEY

ANSELM
ACADEMIC

Created by the publishing team of Anselm Academic.

Cover image royalty free from *www.istockphoto.com*

The scriptural quotations contained herein are from the New Revised Standard Version of the Bible, Catholic Edition. Copyright © 1993 and 1989 by the Division of Christian Education of the National Council of the Churches of Christ in the United States of America. All rights reserved.

Printed in the United States of America

7054

ISBN 978-1-59982-326-3

To Donald L. Gelpi SJ (1934–2011)

Mentor, Colleague, Friend

Contents

The Example of Moses

One day, after Moses had grown up, he went out to his people and saw their forced labor. He saw an Egyptian beating a Hebrew, one of his kinsfolk. He looked this way and that, and seeing no one he killed the Egyptian and hid him in the sand.

— Exodus 2:11–12

MOSES' CONVERSION

Just about everyone who has ever attended church or synagogue on a regular basis is familiar with the story of Moses: A Hebrew baby hidden in the bulrushes because of pharaoh's decree to kill all the boys born to the people enslaved in Egypt, he was discovered by pharaoh's daughter and raised as a member of the royal household. At some point (the scriptures don't say how or when), he realized that he was Hebrew, not Egyptian. Over time he came to understand the brutality inflicted on his people; he killed an Egyptian overseer for beating a Hebrew slave and, consequently, abandoned his privileged position, fled for his life to the desert, and took on the mantle of his true heritage. After some time, despite profound reluctance, he returned to Egypt as God's messenger, demanding that pharaoh release the Hebrews and leading his people on a long journey to the Promised Land.

There is more to his story of conversion than this—his conversion and subsequent attempt to fulfill the will of God is full of complications and even contradictions. At the beginning of the story Moses is unsure of himself. When he sees the Egyptian striking his Hebrew kinsman, he first looks to make sure that no one is around

(Ex 2:12). After he kills the Egyptian, he tries to hide him and then goes home hoping that his act will not be discovered. The next day when he comes upon two Hebrew slaves fighting with each other he becomes angry with them. Rather than embrace Moses for his act of solidarity the men denounce him. Filled with fear of pharaoh and the consequences of his action, Moses flees from Egypt and goes into hiding (Ex 2:15). His actions were not bold, brave, and decisive, neither did they affect any real or structural change in the life of his kinspeople. It was only through a long and complex process of transformation that Moses is able to lead his people to liberation.

Many lessons can be drawn from the story of Moses, but one of the foremost is an understanding of the process of conversion. In the United States, *conversion* is most often associated with *being born again* into believing in Christ, but *conversion* in its broadest sense encompasses the decisive abandonment of one-belief system in order to fully embrace another, whether the belief system is political, social, religious, or even scientific. As the tale of Moses unfolds, the reader observes that his first conversion is not religious at all: he converts from understanding himself as a royal Egyptian to knowing himself as an enslaved Hebrew, from identifying with the Egyptian overseers to becoming one with his fellow Hebrews. Only much later, after he has crossed the desert to Midian, does Moses experience what might be called a religious conversion: when the story says he approaches a "burning" bush and hears God speaking directly to him (Ex 2:23–4:17). In the biblical account, God's self-revelation to Moses changes him profoundly for it sets him on a fundamentally new and unexpected path. God speaks to Moses to give him a mission, a difficult and dangerous task: leadership of and service to others who were so oppressed that they could not organize themselves nor speak on their own behalf, let alone assert their right to freedom. Moses at first hesitates to accept what God is asking of him and doubts his ability to fulfill the task that God sets before him. In time however, Moses accepts his experience of God and authenticates his religious conversion by accepting the mission God asks of him and trusting in the providential care of God to see to its fulfillment. This is the example that Moses has provided down through the millennia.

Nowadays Christians typically think of conversion, if they think of it at all, in only two scenarios: the conversion of adherents of other faiths to Christianity, and the conversion from lukewarm church-goer to fervent believer in Jesus Christ as Lord and Savior. Such ideas of conversion concern only the internal—that is, what a person experiences inside, in the soul or "heart"—as if that is all that matters. Conversion of the soul is certainly a profound event, but it is life-changing only if it leads to different ways of interacting with one's family, friends, neighbors, strangers, and even enemies. Christian conversion means adopting better, more loving ways of relating to others. As the author of the Epistle of James wrote, "Faith by itself, if it has no works, is dead" (Jas 2:17). If a converted person shows no change in behavior, could any change of heart really have taken place?

That writer goes on to indicate what such works should encompass: clothe, feed, shelter, and honor the poor; show no partiality to the rich; and love everyone as much as oneself. In the Gospel account, Jesus, speaking about the last judgment, says that the primary criterion by which God would judge people would be their treatment of those in need. Jesus identifies God's will directly with compassion and care for the hungry, the homeless, the imprisoned, the naked, the outcast: "Just as you did it to one of the least of these who are members of my family, you did it to me" (Mt 25:40). This is exactly what the privileged Moses did in his time, and it is incumbent upon the follower of Christ today to accept God's choice for the poor and the oppressed as one's own people. Embracing God's view of reality, as understood by Christians, may entail profound questioning of the very social arrangements in which one was raised. As the story of Moses shows, such questioning can be dangerous, life altering, because to reject the order of things means that one must reject the many rewards and gratifications that come through the existing order. Such a course of action will likely bring one into conflict with those people who continue to benefit from things as they are.

The idea that God might desire a new and different living arrangement for all people comes as a joyful revelation for the oppressed.[1] Those profiting from the current order, on the other hand, may receive this "good" news with fear, shock, or disbelief. Only those such as Moses, who came to a sure trust in the final

---

1. See further Virgil Elizondo, *The God of Incredible Surprises* (Lanham, MD: Rowan and Littlefield, 2004).

and lasting triumph of God's vision of creation, can accept its consequences. Acceptance of this new vision of creation includes a willingness to limit or even forego temporary goods in this life in the sure knowledge that a greater life awaits those who are faithful to God. As the author of the Letter to the Hebrews writes, "By faith Moses . . . refused to be called a son of Pharaoh's daughter, choosing rather to share ill-treatment with the people of God than to enjoy the fleeting pleasures of sin. He considered abuse . . . to be greater wealth than the treasures of Egypt, for he was looking ahead to the reward" (Heb 11:24–26). Conversion elicits a change of loyalty, the immediate consequences of which may be difficult, painful, or bleak. In the biblical account, Moses transfers his loyalty from pharaoh and Egypt's ruling elite to the oppressed Hebrew people—his "true people"—even though legally and culturally he was entitled to benefit from his status as an heir to the Egyptian throne. The way the story unfolds suggests that Moses came to understand that he had to risk losing his position and his status and all its entitlements in order to bring about the justice that God desired. Only when Moses took this risk could he become one with his people and be truly open to what God was asking of him. Moses' true virtue lay not in his abstract belief in God, but in his concrete decision to see his fate as intrinsically tied to God's love of the downtrodden.

LIBERATION THEOLOGY AND CONVERSION

The story of Moses and the Exodus underscores an important biblical relationship: the relationship between conversion and liberation. In the biblical scheme of things, the liberation of the poor and oppressed is intrinsically tied to the personal and communal conversion of those who are the oppressors. Slavery enslaves not only slaves but also those in power. All people, whether privileged or not, need God's presence in their lives to move beyond the suffocating effects of social structures that enforce discrimination and inequality, that run counter to God's love for creation and the human relationships within it.[2]

---

2. For a further explanation of the sources of this interpretation of the biblical narrative, see Daniel G. Groody, *Globalization, Spirituality and Justice*, (Maryknoll, NY: Orbis, 2007) 31–57.

A theology of liberation underlies much of the biblical narrative and must be embraced to understand the depth of the biblical revelation. Modern-day liberation theology, however, emerged in the twentieth century first in Latin America and then spread to many other regions and groups of people that experienced oppression in their lives.[3] Among economically poor and politically oppressed peoples, liberation theology arises from their despair and their faith that God hears their cries. Liberation theology offers hope to the oppressed and provides them with a way to interpret their struggles and their desire for new life in the midst of suffering and death. Liberation theology has come to represent all those who have ever found themselves in a scandalous condition—the victims of institutional oppression, violence, injustice, and inequity. Liberation theology finds its deepest yearnings and hope in the biblical story of a God who hears the cry of the enslaved Hebrew people and demands that they be set free (Ex 3–15).

This book proposes a spirituality for those "living in pharaoh's house," those who find themselves "inside" of oppressive structures, particularly in the wealthier countries of the world. People of privilege generally do not identify themselves as oppressors, and they usually have no intention whatsoever of being oppressors. That, however, is the problem: too often people who benefit from "things the way they are" live confined and unreflective lives and take for granted the world they have inherited. Liberation theology confronts people with the "way things ought to be," with a strong emphasis on an "option for the poor." By demonstrating how things

---

3. For an explanation of the development of Latin American liberation theology, see further, Roberto Olivaros, "History of Liberation Theology," in Ignacio Ellacuria and Jon Sobrino, eds., *Mysterium Liberationis: Fundamental Concepts of Liberation Theology*, (Maryknoll, NY: Orbis Press, 1993), 3–32; Leonardo and Clodovis Boff, *Introducing Liberation Theology* (Maryknoll, NY: Orbis Press, 1987); Gustavo Gutiérrez, *A Theology of Liberation: History, Politics and Salvation* (Maryknoll, NY: Orbis Press, 1988), 3–61; José Miguez Bonino, *Toward a Christian Political Ethics*, (Philadelphia: Fortress Press, 1983). For an introduction to some other liberation theologies, see especially James Cone, *A Black Theology of Liberation* (Maryknoll, NY: Orbis Press, 1990), Catherine LaCugna, ed., *Freeing Theology: The Essentials of Theology in a Feminist Perspective* (San Francisco: Harper, 1993); Peter Phan, *Christianity with An Asian Face: Asian American Theology in the Making* (Maryknoll, NY: Orbis Press, 2003).

ought to be different, liberation theology begins to break down the cycle of oppression.

However, liberation theology can be a pure abstraction to those who benefit from institutional injustice, for they do not really feel the need for a theology of liberation; instead, they need a theology of conversion. In North America in particular, many need to be converted from the cultural belief that self-centered individualism is not only morally acceptable but also morally necessary for achieving the common good. Many need "new eyes" and "new ears" to see and hear and experience the world in a radically different way: the way that the majority of the world's population experiences it on a daily and routine basis. For that to happen, only a true conversion will suffice: a radical reorientation and reintegration of one's life and priorities.

As part of such a conversion, many need to be liberated from a fundamentally flawed value system. The following chapters of this book will examine this false value system and the ways in which it confuses the idea of "goodness" with human desires and habits that are unhealthy, dangerous, and destructive. This value system enmeshes people in a worldwide system that is often oppressive and even violent on their behalf, without them even realizing it. Several underlying and interconnected beliefs make up the "walls" of pharaoh's house, creating conditions of moral blindness that keep the privileged locked inside a place from which they are unable to engage the world ethically, because they simply do not know that world exists.

Embracing a new vision of reality entails not just individual conversion, but also conversion of societies and initial and ongoing conversions in all dimensions of their collective lives. Part of the process is to discern the inauthentic or distorted aspects of cultures that are in need of fundamental reorientation.

Most forms of liberation theology start by evaluating and identifying economic and cultural structures that by their very nature promote inequality or marginalization. This book proposes a somewhat different starting point: the need to identify and examine underlying cultural misinterpretations of the good. This examination will show that many people have developed an inverted value system and misdirected their desire to create a good life and will yield insights about how people can reorient their values and achieve an ethically good social life.[4]

The initial goal of a cultural or societal conversion is to tear down the walls separating the insiders from the outsiders, the haves from the have-nots. The goal is not primarily to force a redistribution of wealth or power (although that might be a desirable outcome) but to facilitate a solidarity between people who have never known one another, let alone connected on some personal level. With personal connection comes familiarity and affinity, caring and sharing. When genuine solidarity among all members of a society—no matter which side of the wall they happen to be from—develops, it can lead to an understanding that every member has an obligation toward every other member, particularly the poor, weak, and vulnerable. When this reorientation happens, both "insiders" and "outsiders" are set free from enslaving structures.

If it is to happen, the process of critique, conversion, and collaboration will be lengthy and painful on both sides. It would be impossible to convert all of society in one fell swoop; but small communities that are in deep solidarity and communion with ever-widening bonds of universal solidarity can become the model for wider changes.

OUTLINE OF THIS BOOK

The first part of the book, chapters 2–4, will examine the underlying foundations of "the walls of Pharaoh's house": three interrelated and interconnected false interpretations of reality that are set in place as preeminent cultural values. These are precisely the values that have so inverted and distorted the US cultural milieu. These three issues serve as the source and matrix of many other cultural

---

4. There are number of significant studies on culture and its relationship to theological formulation. See especially Bernhard Lonergan, *Method in Theology* (New York: Herder and Herder, 1972); Louis Luzbetak, *The Church and Cultures: New Perspectives in Missiological Anthropology* (Mayknoll: Orbis Books, 1996), especially pp. 133–373; Robert J. Schreiter, *The New Catholicity: Theology between Global and Local* (Maryknoll, NY: Orbis Press, 1997), especially pp. 28–61; Steven B. Bevans, *Models of Contextual Theology*, (Maryknoll, NY: Orbis Press, 1992); and for an overall discussion of culture, see Kathryn Tanner, *Theories of Culture: A New Agenda for Theology*, (Minneapolis, MN: Augsburg Fortress Press, 1997).

ills and a generally false and misguided social ethos. This first part of the book addresses three fundamental issues: (1) radical individualism and the palliative culture that it spawns, (2) the systematic elevation of envy as a virtue in free-market capitalism and the consumerism and materialism that this envy creates, and (3) the optimistic and "positive thinking" façade of a culture that masks that it is ultimately spiritually vacuous and hopeless about the future. Radical individualism and systematic envy lead to pervasive fear, nihilism, and hopelessness in the dominant culture. At the heart of this culture is a profound emptiness that yearns to be filled. A liberating theology must offer something more than the temporary therapeutic palliatives, materialistic distractions, and self-serving ideological rhetoric that American society now provides to its spiritually impoverished members.

The second part of the book, chapters 5–7, defines conversion and examines some of its implications for personal and communal living. To enable this, the text examines the pioneering work of Don Gelpi S.J. Gelpi spent thirty years developing a systematic theology focused exclusively on enculturating the Roman Catholic theological tradition in terms of North American patterns of thought, culture, and social structures.[5] Along these lines, he developed a theology and process of conversion as the centerpiece of his system. His theology of conversion, especially in terms of specifically North American habits of thinking and behaving, serves as a foundational tool for anyone who wants to think seriously about spirituality and the process of conversion. The text then argues that Gelpi's understanding of conversion serves well as part of an overall strategy for creating a liberating spirituality in the North American context.

As a critical aspect of conversion in the US context, the text will evaluate the unique "problem of God" that the American cultural milieu evokes. According to many studies, the United States is a very religious country.[6] Most polls taken in the United States in the last fifty years indicate that more than 90 percent of respondents claim to

---

5. The term *North American* is used in this text to refer to a cultural milieu that is wider than the boundaries of the United States but that is dominated by the United States politically, economically, and socially.

6. See further "Global Index of Religion and Atheism," (WIN-Gallup International, 2012); "American Piety in the 21st Century: New Insights Into the Depth and Complexity of Religion in the US," Baylor Religious Survey (Baylor University: Baylor Institute for Studies of Religion, 2006).

believe in God or some "higher power."[7] In addition, nine out of ten Americans profess to pray at least once a week. In the United States, therefore (unlike in Europe), the problem of God is not really *if* God exists but rather *which* God exists. While the vast majority of Americans believe in God, it is not clear from their responses to polls or their own behaviors whether they share a common understanding of God or God's relationship to human life and history. It is important to examine the unique genesis of American religiosity and determine the common strands and distinct visions that operate within the US understanding of God.

The text then argues that for Christians the notion of the "option for the poor" should serve as the primary measure for authenticating religious conversion. The option for the poor is the practical ethical consequence of belief in the coming of the reign of God. How one treats the poor and those that are outcasts—*anawim* (the Hebrew word for the marginated members of a community)—in any society is the practical test of the level of genuine holistic personal conversion one has undergone. Furthermore, how a society treats its poor, weak, vulnerable, and most despised members serves as a practical test of that society's level of spiritual/moral/ethical well-being and health. Eventually, this practical test must extend beyond the society's national boundaries.

The third part of this book, chapters 8–9, identifies some alternatives and resources within the culture including its intellectual and religious traditions that could counteract and challenge this matrix of overly privatized, materialistic, and superficial values. The result of authentic Christian conversion is mission. All the great Christian traditions of spirituality integrate personal conversion with a sense of mission: service to some segment of society that lives "outside the walls." Articulating a uniquely American vision of the good life can motivate converted Christians to profound social and political engagement on behalf of the good and in service to the *anawim*. This vision must be practical, theologically grounded, rooted in experience, and mindful of the underlying tenets or expectations that most Americans share.

---

7. See "Global Index of Religion and Atheism" and "American Piety in the 21st Century." See also Gallup News Service, *Values and Beliefs—Final Topline*, Gallup Poll Social Series (Timberline: 927914, G: 788, Princeton Job #: 11-05-009; Jeff Jones, Lydia Saad), May 5–8, 2011, and the website for the Pew Forum on Religion and Public Life at *www.pewform.org*.

It must also press beyond a narrow provincialism and connect the North American cultural milieu with the rest of the world in which it is completely enmeshed. Most of all, this spirituality must offer liberating hope to those who find themselves trapped inside the walls of power and privilege. It must also challenge to conversion those who do not yet know they are imprisoned. Finally, Christians united in their desire to imitate Christ, struggling together against injustice, poverty, war, and for the greater good of all, can help to fill the deep void at the heart of US culture.

QUESTIONS FOR REFLECTION

1. What preconceptions come to mind when you hear the word *conversion*? Are these preconceptions positive or negative? Are you familiar with conversion as a religious concept? Explain.

2. Is there a prevailing understanding of what constitutes goodness in the United States? Do you agree with the chapter's premise that many people have an understanding of good that is rooted in an inadequate value system? Why or why not?

3. What unjust social, political, or economic conditions are present in your local community or your state? How do these unjust structures affect you? Do you benefit from any unjust social, political, or economic structures?

4. Identify the most valuable and most problematic aspects of US culture?

5. Identify any aspects of the North American cultural milieu that may have you "walled in" or "walled off" from seeing the world as it truly is.

FOR FURTHER READING

Butler, Jon, Grant Wacker, and Randall Balmer, *Religion in American Life: A Short History* (Oxford: Oxford University Press, 2008).

Elizondo, Virgil, *The God of Incredible Surprises* (Lanham, MD: Rowman and Littlefield, 2004).

Gallagher, Michael Paul, *Clashing Symbols: An Introduction to Faith and Culture* (New York: Paulist Press, 2004).

Niebuhr, H. Richard, *Christ and Culture* (New York: Harper & Row, 1951).

Tanner, Kathryn, *Theories of Culture: A New Agenda for Theology* (Minneapolis MN: Augsburg Fortress Press, 1997).

Taylor, Charles, *The Secular Age* (Boston: Belknap Press, 2007).

Wuthnow, Robert, *American Mythos: Why Our Best Efforts to Be a Better Nation Fall Short* (Princeton: Princeton University Press, 2006).

2

The First Wall of Pharaoh's House

Individualism

"To thine own self be true."

— POLONIUS IN SHAKESPEARE'S *HAMLET*[1]

HOW PEOPLE BECOME "WALLED IN"

Chapter 1 proposed that a nexus of foundational and interconnected beliefs make up the "walls" of pharaoh's house, often creating conditions for a kind for moral blindness These walls can be said to blind people because they keep the privileged locked inside a limited vision or interpretation of reality that prevents them from authentically and ethically "seeing" and engaging the world. This book offers an initial analysis of some of the walls that seem to enclose members of the US cultural ethos. This analysis is neither exhaustive nor does it imply that the US culture is somehow more deficient or sinful than any other culture. Nevertheless, one must begin with some analysis of the limited and negative elements of the culture in order to discover plausible ways to dismantle walls. One such wall that suffuses the US social ethos is a kind of radical individualism that places one's personal happiness and well-being above all other considerations.

Writing about the unique contribution of the Roman Catholic perspective to her work, Flannery O'Connor once stated, "The

---

1. William Shakespeare, *Hamlet*, Act 1, Scene 3.

Catholic novelist believes that you destroy your freedom by sin; the modern reader believes, I think, that you gain it in that way."[2] Many Americans have come to believe in the right to personal happiness at any cost, valuing this belief above all else. Furthermore, many believe they can achieve this goal only through an individual quest that often subverts the very end they are trying to achieve. Much contemporary research indicates that the relentless focus on professional success can ruin the marriages and family life of many couples or can otherwise disconnect them from the friends and communities that are most important to them.[3] The unbridled desire for professional and economic success is often fueled by the uncritical belief that it would lead to happiness. However, it turns out that the cost of success is often the loss of those aspects of life that offer the greatest opportunity for meaning, intimacy, and love. Unfortunately, only late in life do people discover that success and happiness are not necessarily the same, and that one often contradicts the other.[4]

Freedom, in the American context, often means freedom *from* something. In a positive sense, this emerges from the history of North America. Many of the first immigrants to the "New World" aimed to escape religious persecution and establish communities free from the power of established churches and governments that tried to regulate their beliefs. Later, people living in the thirteen colonies broke off from Great Britain's colonial system, desiring freedom to control and govern their own destiny. Later still, the struggle against Britain to establish an independent government gave way to an internal struggle over slavery. This debate over the true meaning of freedom, in a country founded largely on this ideal, led eventually to a civil war that resulted in freedom for both the enslaved and their masters from the scourge of an inhuman and dehumanizing institution. Subsequent US cultural history has been dominated by a desire to expand the

---

2. Flannery O'Connor, *Mystery and Manners*, eds. Sally and Robert Fitzgerald (New York: Farrar, Straus & Giroux, 1962), 116.

3. For a more detailed analysis of this phenomenon in US life, see Shawn Achor, *The Happiness Advantage: The Seven Principles of Positive Psychology That Fuel Success and Performance at Work*, (New York: Crown Business, 2010). He in turn cites studies by a number of other sources but particularly the work of Martin E. P. Seligman, and especially *Authentic Happiness: Using the New Positive Psychology to Realize Your Potential for Lasting Fulfillment* (New York: Atria Press, 2003).

4. Achor, *The Happiness Advantage*, 37–45.

understanding of freedom, to establish and broaden the definition of civil rights in a number of areas of social life, and to spread the ideal of freedom to other nations and regions of the world.

In a negative sense though, freedom understood exclusively as *freedom from* can also come to imply freedom from essential dimensions of personal and social development, *from* the bonds that create and sustain communal life and personal development, *from* a just social order that might limit a relentless pursuit of personal fortune, *from* the religious vision of a final judgment that will hold people individually and communally accountable for their actions either for or against God's plan for creation. The Christian worldview to which O'Connor refers would instead hold that genuine freedom is freedom *for* something rather than *from* something. Authentic human freedom, according to the Christian view, is freedom *for* love, freedom *for* service to others, freedom *for* long-term bonds of community that require personal self-sacrifice and the power to forgive, freedom *for* a profound relationship with the Spirit of God that heals, invigorates, and transforms individuals and communities; it is the freedom to join with God in co-creating the universe according to God's own vision.

The lack of human freedom to which O'Connor alludes has its roots in a fundamental misunderstanding of reality that keeps people from doing the good they want to do (Rom 7:14–20) and that causes even good people to do bad things. The twentieth century was replete with examples of seemingly ordinary and even "good" people caught up in horrible and destructive ideologies—Nazism, fascism, and Stalinism across Europe; racism, sexism, and classism in the United States and Great Britain—that killed, displaced, and ostracized untold millions of innocent people. That ordinary people, perceived as living morally good and even praiseworthy personal lives, can get caught up in inhuman forms of evil without consciously realizing they are doing anything wrong constitutes one of the abiding mysteries of human existence. The seeming inability of ordinary people to often distinguish good from evil characterizes what the Christian tradition means by original sin. A full understanding of the concept of original sin requires study of both theological and experiential interpretations.

Theologically, original sin is grounded in the biblical narrative of humanity's inability to sustain a faithful relationship with God. The story of Adam and Eve's fall in the Garden of Eden (Gen 3) can be interpreted as a metaphor for humankind's fundamental unwillingness to obey and live according to the order God originally designed for the world.[5] This interpretation of original sin presupposes that "natural" human life is in need of redemption by the Creator because a foundational rupture has occurred and still exists in the life-giving and life-sustaining relationship between God and humanity.[6] The level and extent of this rupture has generated a great deal of theological reflection and divergence of opinion over the centuries, but most Christian theologians seem to agree on the reality that the term *original sin* denotes.

The American theologian Reinhold Niebuhr maintained that original sin was the only Christian doctrine that is empirically verifiable—that is, that it is an observable phenomenon and must be accounted for in any thoughtful analysis of human social systems.[7] Practically speaking, the concept of original sin conveys both a sociological reality and a psychological insight. Humans are born into a fundamentally sinful world in which institutionalized and structural injustice and violence all too often characterize cultural and social situations. Such injustice and violence are institutional and structural because they are not the result of any one person's or group's decisions but have arisen from previous historical practices of injustice. In aggregate, these unjust practices have created communal habits, patterns of "normal" human relationships that diminish and damage the people who participate in them.

It is important to note here that humans are not born with their personalities and moral values already set. Children learn from their

---

5. For a traditional theological account of original sin, see Karl Rahner, "Original Sin," in *Sacramentum Mundi*, ed. Karl Rahner et al. (New York: Herder and Herder, 1969), 4:331; or Gabriel Daly, "Original Sin," in *The New Dictionary of Theology*, ed. Joseph Komonchak, Mary Collins, and Dermott A. Lane (Collegeville, MN: Liturgical Press, 1988), 727–28; for an alternative account, see also Phyllis Trible, "Eve and Adam: Genesis 2–3 Reread," *Andover Newton Quarterly* 13, no.4 (March 1973): 251–58.

6. See Karl Rahner, "The Sin of Adam," in *Theological Investigations*, trans. David Bourke (New York: Crossroad, 1982), 11:249–50.

7. See further Reinhold Niebuhr, *The Children of Light and the Children of Darkness* (New York: Charles Scribner's Sons, 1944) 16–17; Robert McAfee Brown, ed., *The Essential Reinhold Niebuhr*, (New Haven: Yale University Press, 1986), 168–77.

environment and gradually integrate external moral codes of conduct, customs, and manners as they grow and develop. Each person is shaped by a complex social process that includes both a kind of assimilation of the person into the actions of the whole and the direct imitation of others.[8] In this sense, by adulthood people generally reflect the cultural values and social customs of their families and the larger society in which they were raised. That is not to say that individuals have no choice in their own development; indeed, humans often face choices between competing values and expectations *within* their own cultural and communal milieu. The choices a person must make, combined with things such as their genetic predispositions and psychological factors, mean that each person will be unique even if shaped by the same cultural values and customs as others.

Communities and societies, like the individuals that comprise them, are not perfect. Societies cannot escape the influence of false values, irrational prejudices, unjust social and economic structures, and dangerous tendencies to coercion and violence. Societies can embody modes of corporate sinfulness, just as individuals can harbor sinful tendencies and vices. Because individuals are born into existing communities and socialized into their values and ways of living, sinful tendencies are passed along just as readily as loving tendencies. Humans will often take on the negative and sinful elements of a society as unconsciously and directly as they will many other attitudes and modes of behavior.[9] This social process creates individuals who not only interpret the world through disordered and unjust social structures but also ratify and advance these structures through beliefs they have adopted as their own, habits they follow, and every personal choice they may make. Born into societies affected by sin, humans inevitably endorse and embody through their ways of living, views of reality that too often mistake evil and sin for good.

The prevalence of racism in American culture shows how this social process operates. The US social historian George Fredrickson

---

8. See the social psychologist George Herbert Mead, *Mind, Self, and Society*, in *Works of George Herbert Mead*, vol. 1, ed. Charles W. Morris (Chicago: University of Chicago Press, 1934), especially 186–92.

9. Cf. Donald Gelpi, *The Gracing of Human Experience: Rethinking the Relationship between Nature and Grace* (Collegeville, MN: Liturgical Press, 2001), 321–26.

defines *racism* as "when one ethnic group or historical collectivity dominates, excludes, or seeks to eliminate another on the basis of differences that it believes are hereditary and unalterable."[10] In the United States four hundred years of extreme social injustice created an environment in which even well-intentioned people cannot evade the weight of history. Stereotypical images, denigrating prejudices, social avoidance, outright segregation, and the fundamental, though often barely perceptible, barriers that define race relationships are the legacy of hundreds of years of outright persecution and de facto genocide. These social evils lie so deep in the communal consciousness that even the racial groups affected by them often take them on as the "normal" way that life should be.[11]

At the time that the lofty ideals of the Declaration of Independence were being articulated about the universal and inalienable rights of humans, the presence of African slaves was growing in America and empowering an economic boom that would last for another eighty years. Simultaneously, native people were being systematically removed from their lands and herded like animals across the country to reservations where they wouldn't interfere with expanding, largely European, immigration into America. Even after the US Civil War, African Americans, though technically freed from bondage, were kept from experiencing full citizenship in the Southern states for a hundred years.

In these same years, African Americans in the Northern states were systematically discriminated against, segregated, and forced to endure humiliations solely because of the color of their skin. Immigrants who arrived in the United States after the turn of twentieth century experienced waves of anti-immigrant hatred and discrimination based on their socioeconomic class or religious status. Even after the dramatic developments and advancements of the civil rights era in the 1960s and '70s, racial prejudice and "white privilege" continued to affect social relations in the United

---

10. George Fredrickson, "The Historical Origins and Development of Racism," from an essay for the PBS documentary, *Race: The Power of an Illusion*, 2003 (*www.pbs. org/race/000_About/002_04-background-02-01.htm*). This in turn derives from his book *Racism: A Short History*, (Princeton: Princeton University Press, 2002).

11. Robert Coles, *Children of Crisis: A Study of Courage and Fear*, (Boston: Atlantic-Little, Brown, 1967).

States.[12] Anti-immigrant sentiment and hostile racism revived at the end of the twentieth century with the dramatic increase in Hispanic/Latino immigrants, and especially the intense debate surrounding the basic dignity of those immigrants who entered the country illegally yet served as the backbone of a thriving US service economy.[13] To inform a full portrait of this sad underside of American history, one could also look to the experiences of Asian Americans and Arab Americans, who report numerous analogous stories of ill treatment and discrimination based on often unconscious racist stereotypes and presumptions.

The prevalence of racism in American culture serves as a reminder that the good intentions of individual people or even a generation of well-intentioned people cannot seem to undo or counterbalance the prejudices deeply embedded in the ways many Americans have learned to interpret reality. A fundamental conversion at both a personal and communal level will require repentance and a myriad of habitual and social structural changes over generations. This type of radical reorientation and transformation of individuals and society constitutes the only real solution to the racist presuppositions of American society. Racism serves as only one dimension of what could be termed the original sin that walls ordinary people inside a false value system and misguided interpretation of what is normal and even moral.

FIRST WALL: RADICAL INDIVIDUALISM

Radical individualism represents another form of original sin at the heart of US social life. Individuality itself connotes a "good" at the very root of American culture because the founders of the United States set out, in a very admirable way, to respect the rights of the individual. American culture, however, has always struggled with two models of how one achieves authentic individuality; that is, how one develops and lives as a unique and autonomous

---

12. See further Paula S. Rothenberg, *White Privilege: Essential Readings on the Other Side of Racism* (New York: Worth Publishers, 2002).

13. See further Daniel G. Groody, *Border of Death, Valley of Life: An Immigrant Journey of Heart and Spirit* (Lanham, MD: Rowan & Littlefield, 2002).

person capable of taking responsibility for his or her decisions and actions. One model corresponds to the traditional Christian pattern in which a person becomes an authentic individual through a process of conversion and discipleship most profoundly articulated in the teachings of Jesus and the theology of Saint Paul. The other, referred to here as radical individualism, is grounded in the Enlightenment philosophy of Thomas Hobbes (1588–1679), John Locke (1632–1704), and Immanuel Kant (1724–1804) as well as in the distinctively American tradition of economic, social, and psychological theory.

Radical individualism in America today is really the product of three concepts: utilitarian individualism, expressive individualism, and pragmatism. Utilitarian individualism, stemming from the philosophies of the Enlightenment[14] and classically expressed in the works of US founding father Benjamin Franklin (1706–1790), is based on the belief that the highest good of the whole is achieved when each individual reaches his or her own highest potential. Although the most obvious context is financial, the concept extends to other areas. Expressive individualism, as American sociologist Robert Bellah (1927–) and his coauthors point out in their book *Habits of the Heart: Individualism and Commitment and American Life*,[15] came to the fore through the writing and reputation of the American poet, journalist, and essayist Walt Whitman (1819–1892). This strand of individualism is based on the belief that each person should, as much as possible and regardless of the costs, pursue, cultivate, and express whatever aspect of one's creative and imaginative interior life one is disposed to engage. Finally, pragmatism, of the kind that American philosopher and psychologist William James (1842–1910) advocated, is essentially the belief that truth is not something fixed and eternal that we can know with certainty but, in

---

14. The Enlightenment generally refers to the philosophical and cultural period of seventeenth and eighteenth century in Europe and the North American colonies. The period was characterized by the rise of "reason" and scientific method as primary modes of analyzing all dimensions of political, economic, and social life. For a further exploration and analysis of this period, see Louis Dupre, *The Enlightenment and the Intellectual Foundations of Modern Culture* (New Haven: Yale University Press, 2005).

15. Robert Bellah et al., *Habits of the Heart: Individualism and Commitment in American Life* (San Francisco: Harper & Row, 1985), 32–35.

fact, changes and develops in response to the actual life experience of each person.[16] The realm of truth is centered in the person who must define it to some extent for herself or himself.

According to Bellah, individualism, in the American context, is premised on the belief that each individual is a personal moral universe.[17] Each person is responsible for determining what is best for him or her, and then working for self-fulfillment. What is best for each person depends on that person: no other reality can dictate or even shape the needs and possibilities of each. The good is basically defined as one's personal preferences.

One way to contrast the two models of how to exist in society—for the common good vs. for the good of self—is to look at how the task of becoming an individual has been portrayed in two very popular twentieth-century American movies: *The Wizard of Oz* and *Home Alone.*

The Wizard of Oz was the highest-grossing film of 1939, a year filled with great movies such as *Gone with the Wind, Mr. Smith Goes to Washington, Of Mice and Men, Ninotchka, Stagecoach,* and *Goodbye, Mr. Chips,* among others. Based on the L. Frank Baum story, *The Wizard of Oz* tells of a young girl who is torn from her family and town and must find her way back home. Along the way, she joins with a small community of others who also have problems and struggles and who cannot seem to find their way home. So they travel together, sharing their resources and talents, and through struggles and difficulties, they discover things about themselves they never knew. Ultimately, they come to understand that any talents they might possess are only of value if they can be of service to the other members of their community.

Dorothy, the main character, is the very model of genuine individuality: she is just a little girl when she leaves Kansas but returns with the maturity to undertake new responsibilities in the life of her family and her community. Her experience shows

---

16. There are many different types of American pragmatism. For an analysis of the different strains of pragmatism in American philosophy, see John E. Smith, *The Spirit of American Philosophy* (Oxford: Oxford University Press, 1963), and H. O. Mounce, *The Two Pragmatisms* (Routledge: New York, 1997).

17. Bellah, 142–43.

that the process of maturing is a journey that is *shared*: people discover who they are meant to be and what talents they have precisely because others join them and help them to see themselves more clearly.

Fifty years later, the highest-grossing film of the year was *Home Alone*. Celebrating the rugged individualism that dates back to the very founding of the United States, stories such as *Home Alone* have always had a place in American lore and film—just as films like *The Wizard of Oz*, extolling the power of friendship and disparate individuals united against a common problem or foe still serve as fundamental fare in American cinema. Most often, Hollywood set the tale of rugged individualism on the frontier, where a single man (always a male) was on his own and shaped both his destiny and that of others through his strength and courage. In movies such as *The Magnificent Seven, Shane, High Noon, High Plains Drifter, Butch Cassidy and the Sundance Kid,* and *Dances with Wolves,* this man (or small group of men) was the stranger, the loner, the truly self-possessed individual. *Home Alone,* in 1990, simply builds upon this tradition; it is the story of a little boy, Kevin McCallister, who is left to his own devices to defend himself and his home from attack when his family absentmindedly leaves on vacation without him. With ingenuity and growing self-empowerment, he saves himself from both criminals and an absent community and in doing so learns extreme self-reliance. Though he's but eight years old, he comes to realize that he cannot depend on his family or his community to defend him in his time of need.

Diagnosing the Consequences of Being *Home Alone*

In his book *Bowling Alone in America: The Collapse and Revival of American Community,*[18] Harvard sociologist Robert Putnam systematically examines what he calls the decline of "social capital" in American culture over the last forty years. By *social capital* Putnam means a sense of civic mindedness among community members that

---

18. Robert D. Putnam, *Bowling Alone in America: The Collapse and Revival of American Community* (New York: Simon & Schuster, 2000).

is embedded in a "dense network of reciprocal social relations."[19] The breadth and strength of these networks indicates how much individuals have "invested" in the growth, development, and well-being of the communities in which they live and upon which they depend for their livelihood and personal fulfillment.

Putnam makes a distinction between "bonding" communities and "bridging" communities. He defines bonding communities as ordinarily exclusive and tending to be inward looking—communities that reinforce exclusive, homogeneous identities such as ethnic-based organizations, country clubs, bridge clubs, or other groups for people with similar interests or problems. Bridging communities, on the other hand, are inclusive groups that attempt to bring diverse individuals together to enhance the common good at some level. Civil rights movements, ecumenical groups, and citizen's alliances are examples of bridging communities. Some communities can function both ways: for example, the Rotary Club, parent-teacher organizations, the Red Cross, and many "fraternal organizations" such as Kiwanis and the Lions Club bring a variety of individuals together to work for social betterment. Putnam contends that any healthy society will have a lively mix of both bonding and bridging communities, and both types of groups will call forth a high degree of social capital from their participants.

Putnam's careful analysis of end-of-the-twentieth-century American society revealed what he called a "shared sense of civic malaise"[20] that had already led to a frightening loss of social capital at almost every level in American life. Putnam finds that there has been a profoundly steep decline in American participation in bridging communities and a mixed and unclear relationship between individuals and bonding communities. This breakdown in community life along with the underlying radical individualism seems, to him, to be a danger to the future of American society. In his view, it is the key issue facing Americans at the dawn of the twenty-first century.

Putnam's research reinforces and expands upon the work done fifteen years previously by a group of sociologists at the University of California under the direction of Robert Bellah. Their book

---

19. Ibid., 19; Bellah, *Habits of the Heart*, 32–35.

20. Putnam, *Bowling Alone in America*, 25.

previously mentioned, *Habits of the Heart*,[21] paints a picture of a dominant American ethos that is overwhelmingly controlled by the need to free oneself from all external constraints. To be free of any limits on one's self-expression is seen as the highest good, as the ultimate goal of human striving. Such desire for complete self-fulfillment makes community life increasingly irrelevant for the "dominant culture," which Bellah defines as the white, middle- and upper-middle-class elites that "set the tone" and control the popular and public agenda and discourse in American life. Of course, various subcultures resist and even rebel against the dominant culture, but the dominant culture does subtly subvert and infiltrate all levels of American life and can often undermine the best interests of particular subcultures.[22]

The Palliative Culture

If individualism is the leitmotif of American culture—the theme around which the matrix of the culture revolves—then society cultivates the concept and responds to the needs it creates. When the dominant ideal is radical individualism, culture's role is to provide an environment that meets the needs of individuals for full self-determination and self-expression, at least as much as is possible given the total needs of the society. American culture is thus "palliative." *Palliative* is a word that derives from a Latin root that means to "cloak" or "cover up." Its contemporary usage primarily refers to a medical process in which the attempt is to treat the symptoms of a disease or illness rather than cure or heal the root cause of the problem. Palliative care often refers to end-of-life treatment in which the goal is to make the patient comfortable and free from pain when going through the final stages of life.

American culture is thus palliative in two ways: On the one hand, this culture does not exist for itself, neither is it good in itself. Rather, it serves as a medium for individuals to seek whatever they feel is good for them. Society helps people to find their own level of

---

21. Ibid., 100.

22. For good examples of subcultures that do not fit this profile, see Dean Hoge, William Dinges, Mary Johnson, and Juan L. Gonzales Jr., *Young Adult Catholics: Religion in the Culture of Choice* (Notre Dame, IN: University of Notre Dame Press, 2001), 113–30.

liberty, happiness, and comfort. It also coordinates competing interests to ensure maximum self-expression for each individual. Society does not function to achieve some higher good (such as improved social conditions or the common good) but to improve the quality of life of each person separately.[23]

On the other hand, individualism is tough and takes a real toll on many people. Many need to be treated for symptoms of a sadness, depression, and emotional dysfunction that are a kind of "side effect" of living in a radically individualistic milieu. A Harris Interactive Poll conducted in 2004 found that 27 percent of Americans had participated in some form of mental health treatment in the prior two years.[24] In his book *American Therapy: The Rise of Psychotherapy in the United* States, Jonathan Engel indicates that over the course of their lives roughly 50 percent of Americans will undergo some form of psychotherapy. The need, which individualism gives rise to, for people to be fully independent and self-determining in all areas of life is a burden that can strain their mental health. Often, the more people try to control their lives, the more dependent they become on society to enable this process and to ameliorate its side effects. A great deal of energy and resources—social conventions, expectations, educational systems, government, even the economy—are geared toward making the ideal of individualism possible and dealing with its effects when it succeeds.

At a social level, it is the role of society to give each person as much freedom as possible to delineate needs and create his or her own world. Society has no real means of reconciling conflicting claims to truth as any claims are seen as a matter of personal preference. Such preferences can take on a kind of normative or patterned quality and then become values. Thus the final source of one's values is also ultimately internal: there is no criterion larger than the individual self that either holds one accountable or can inform one's choices. Society cannot sanction one set of "values" over another and exists mainly to maximize each member's self-interest. If society succeeds in supplying this kind of individualistic environment, it is

---

23. Bellah, *Habits of the Heart*, 145.

24. *www.prnewswire.com/news-releases/therapy-in-america-2004-poll-shows—mental-health-treatment-goes-mainstream-73817497.html.*

"working." If society encumbers the individual with social ties and obligations that limit self-expression and impedes self-improvement, then society is "not working."

In the individualistic world being described, the critical task for each individual is to be fully aware of his or her needs, feelings, and desires. People can know their preferences, shape their value systems, and make choices based on their own good only if they have a thorough grasp of the inner life to which they must give expression and fulfillment. In other words, the overriding concern is "How do I really feel about thus and so?" As Bellah states, "The self becomes the crucial site for the comparative examination and probing of feelings that result from utilitarian acts and inspire expressive ones."[25] As a result, the primary moral problems that confront people are basically tactical—how can they juggle all the competing possibilities so as to benefit from as many as possible, while not obstructing or excluding other desires that may arise in the future?

The answer is, they can't. If they can make no decisions, and certainly no commitments, until they have surveyed all possible options and judged all the possible outcomes, they will never reach the end of their questioning. The process of self-discovery is ongoing; people can never know everything about themselves; indeed, individuals change in response to what happens around them. Further, how can they ever be certain which outcome might be in their best interest? Such a determination would require prescience as well as self-knowledge. Nevertheless, they persist, and the process of self-discovery takes precedence over any other activity; it becomes an end in itself, and all commitments outside of the fundamental commitment to self are secondary. Bellah calls this way of thinking the "therapeutic attitude." *Therapy* is the name Bellah gives for this on going process that creates its own world as it goes along, increasingly in isolation from everyone else. The term *palliative therapy*, in distinction from genuine psychotherapy, could be useful here in that it does not seek to get at the root cause of anything or actually bring about a change in the fundamental orientation of the self. It merely tries to make people feel better about patterns of life to which they will continue to adhere.

---

25. Bellah, *Habits of the Heart*, 78.

This type of palliative therapy can undermine interpersonal relationships.[26] Self-sacrifice is never in our best interest and, thus, cannot be part of any legitimate relationship; if a relationship is not mutual, one or both parties are not being true to themselves. This type of relationship requires a kind of self-assertion; one must know what one wants out of the relationship and work in conjunction with the other to meet both parties' autonomous interests. If that is not possible, each person has an obligation to seek a relationship that is more mutually satisfying. In this scenario, "a kind of selfishness is essential to love."[27] As in utilitarian and expressive individualism, if both parties seek their own best interests, the greatest good will automatically result. At the deepest and most intimate personal level in American society, relationship and commitment are understood in legally contractual terms. The palliative therapeutic attitude essentially holds that there are no binding social obligations, and that even the most personal relationships exist only as long as both parties are "happy."

The result is the same when the relationship is between an individual and an institution. People commit themselves to a social group or standard only when it is in their best interests—financial, religious, psychological, social, and so on. This type of thinking has become so pervasive that it is practically unconscious. Bellah calls this aspect of the therapeutic attitude "therapeutic contractualism."[28] There are simply no overriding obligations that automatically have a claim on individuals if they do not or cannot freely choose to commit themselves. Even if they freely enter into a binding obligation, they are free to reevaluate that commitment at any time.

Community, in the traditional sense, becomes very difficult to achieve; what has generally replaced it is a plethora of voluntary associations. These associations are usually organized to satisfy the

---

26. This is not to say that many, many people have not experienced dysfunctional and abusive aspects of relationships (society, church, family, marriage, etc.) and that their retreat into the therapeutic culture does not make sense on a purely practical and psychological level. The dysfunctional and often oppressive elements of institutional life must be acknowledged if valid alternatives to both of these types of relationships and their therapeutic reactions are to be found.

27. Bellah, *Habits of the Heart*, 100.

28. Ibid., 102–7.

needs of a special-interest group or to perform a certain task or social function. Many people join and stay in these groups as long as, and at the level at which, their needs are met. Although these associations can accomplish a great deal of good and even address significant moral issues, their long-term effects and membership are often fleeting. Furthermore, the ideology of radical individualism inculcates many of those who join to expect to "get" something in return for their dedication, even if it is just a good feeling. Often then, if there is no trade-off to justify such commitments, many members will view these organizations as simply external obligations from which they need to be freed.

✳Palliative Spirituality

In the United States, the palliative therapeutic attitude that defines our interpersonal and social relationships extends to God. For many, God is constitutionally optional. Even nonbelievers would hold that if some people need to believe in God to fulfill some existential void in their lives or because it is psychologically advantageous, they are free to do so. Furthermore, even those of us who believe in God often see the relationship in therapeutic, contractual terms. If God wants what is best for humans, God wants humans to be healthy and happy, so God desires what they do. Humans equate their individual quest for fulfillment with the will of God. Any external codes of conduct or absolutely binding moral obligations to something that they did not personally choose are seen as distortions of God's will.

In fact, many people see God as a dimension, or part, of themselves. While some may suspect that God is actually an unhealthy and immature element of the psyche that needs to be fixed, others have observed the Divine become manifest through the growth in wholeness and autonomy of each person. To pray to God is actually to encounter the deepest and most profound part of the self. This process of introspection and self-expression already serves as the primary focus of the process. Instead of drawing individuals out of themselves and into a wider and more important reality, belief in God becomes a divine mandate and a holy quest to find the truth within.

The foregoing description of the palliative therapeutic attitude is not a caricature of any particular spirituality or to create a "straw man" to rail against. Rather, drawing on the research of Bellah and others, it is important to tease out a tendency present in many religious and spiritual movements in US culture.[29] The dominant ethos of any culture will shape its religious expressions. In mainstream US culture, the tendency for religion to fulfill the palliative therapeutic needs of its members is so overwhelming that it reinforces the very self-centeredness that most faiths, including Christianity, are trying to overcome. Religiously inspired commitments to help the oppressed and marginated members of society rarely move beyond abstract organizational statements. In his research, Robert Putnam found that religious communities are more bonding than bridging and that new religious associations do not even recognize the need to act as bridging communities.[30]

Are the problems people face as a society the result of their inability to fully embody the individualism that informs their collective life, or is there something more fundamentally wrong? Is their culture enmeshed in a value system that makes the attainment of full human authenticity and wholeness impossible? Can the fundamental assumptions upon which their culture is based truly sustain them in a healthy way? Is it possible to conceive of an authentic form of spirituality that seeks to truly liberate people in this cultural context that resists the tendency to become individualistic and palliative? These are some of the problems to be addressed as this book moves from analysis to solutions.

CONCLUSION

All societies experience fundamental flaws, or contradictions, at the heart of their social ethos that can wall in or wall off their members from achieving an authentically good life. Christian theology traditionally termed these foundational contradictions as *original sin*. While it is possible to identify multiple types of original sin in the US cultural context, one of the most significant is identified here as radical individualism. Radical individualism derives from the

---

29. See especially Ross Drouthat, *Bad Religion: How We Became a Nation of Heretics* (New York: Free Press, 2012).

30. Putnam, *Bowling Alone in America*, 74–79.

authentic and valuable American cultural value placed on individuality and the significance of the inviolability of the individual and his or her conscience. The American sociologist Robert Bellah and his team of researchers discovered that this fundamental value could be understood in two ways: In one interpretation, individual identity emerges out of the communal and social process of taking responsibility for oneself and others and finding one's unique contribution and, therefore, core identity through sharing one's gifts and talents with other people. This process yields a genuine sense of individuality and personal identity that in turn both builds up the community and requires it to respect the rights and essential dignity of the individual.

In the other interpretation, individuality is interpreted largely through the lens of what Bellah terms "utilitarian and expressive individualism." This concept of individuality raises the status of the individual and his or her personal identity to a practically ideological state of importance. In this model, one achieves individuality precisely by breaking the bonds of community and moving beyond the limits set by social mores to discover one's distinctive personal identity. Here the rights and needs of the individual take precedence over those of society and society is often understood as the most dangerous foe of the quest for individual self-fulfillment. US popular culture has long glorified this interpretation of individuality and has often portrayed the hero as the one who neither needs nor is constrained by the community. This kind of radical individualism sets up each person as a unique and autonomous moral universe and requires that the each person pursue his or her own unique destiny apart from, and often in opposition to, the social and communal ethos in which that person lives.

This type of radical individualism has a severe impact on both the US society and on the individuals that participate in it. By so dramatically elevating the needs of the individual over the needs of the common good and even placing the two in a kind of fundamental opposition, the social structures and communal ties that are essential for any society are greatly strained. The sociologist Robert Putnam and others have documented the decline of US civic and cultural life in the light of the absolute priority of individual rights over the good of the whole. This diminishment of community and the possibilities of social life in turn affect individuals in their quest for self-expression and fulfillment. Individuals, often separated from the very social ties that would enhance their personal lives, find themselves struggling in an environment that both encourages their process of self-discovery and impedes its. These increasingly isolated and disconnected individuals, therefore, experience psychologically painful and even debilitating side effects from the individualism they so heartily embrace. Bellah and others assert that this reality in turn gives rise to a therapeutic or palliative culture that attempts to ameliorate the most negative effects of this struggle and social condition. However, the palliative process, rather than getting to the roots of modern problems and challenging individuals to truly change, offers instead only a partial and superficial respite from the turmoil that individualism itself engenders. This palliative approach simultaneously infects many other dimensions of the culture leading to greater levels of social, political, and even religious dissonance and incoherence. For these reasons, radical individualism represents a central challenge to those who want to offer an authentic and alternative spirituality in the US cultural context.

QUESTIONS FOR REFLECTION

1. If you are familiar with the concept of original sin, consider how the explanation of original sin in this chapter compares with your previous understanding of this concept.

2. Identify types of original sin that seem prevalent in the United States or in your country of origin.

3. Do you see yourself as someone on a quest to attain individuality? Why or why not? What examples or images come to mind when you think of the importance of individuality in US culture?

4. Identify positive and negative effects of the emphasis on individualism in US culture.

5. To what extent do you agree or disagree with the analysis of Bellah and Putnam presented in this chapter?

6. Does your experience resonate with the process of attaining personal identity and purpose described in this chapter? Explain.

FOR FURTHER READING

Achor, Shawn, *The Happiness Advantage: The Seven Principles of Positive Psychology That Fuel Success and Performance at Work* (New York: Crown Business, 2010).

Bellah, Robert, *The Broken Covenant: American Civil Religion in a Time of Trial* (Chicago: University of Chicago Press, 1992).

Bellah, Robert, et al., *Habits of the Heart: Individualism and Commitment in American Life* (San Francisco: Harper & Row, 1985).

———. *Individualism and Commitment in American Life: Readings on the Themes of Habits of the Heart* (New York: Harper & Row, 1987).

Brown, Robert McAfee, ed., *The Essential Reinhold Niebuhr* (New Haven: Yale University Press, 1986).

Coles, Robert, *Children of Crisis: A Study of Courage and Fear* (Boston: Atlantic-Little, Brown, 1967).

Daly, Gabriel, "Original Sin," in *The New Dictionary of Theology*, eds. Joseph Komonchak, Mary, and Dermott A. Lane (Collegeville, MN: Liturgical Press, 1988), 727–28;

Fredrickson, George, *Racism: A Short History* (Princeton: Princeton University Press, 2002).

Groody, Daniel G., *Border of Death, Valley of Life: An Immigrant Journey of Heart and Spirit* (Lanham, MD: Rowan & Littlefield, 2002).

Hoopes, James, *Community Denied: The Wrong Turn of Pragmatic Liberalism* (Ithaca, NY: Cornell University Press, 1998).

Lachs, John, *A Community of Individuals* (New York: Routledge, 2003).

Mead, George Herbert, *Mind, Self, and Society*, in the *Works of George Herbert Mead*, vol. 1, ed. Charles W. Morris (Chicago: University of Chicago Press, 1934).

Niebuhr, Reinhold, *The Children of Light and the Children of Darkness* (New York: Charles Scribner's Sons, 1944).

Putnam, Robert D., *Bowling Alone in America: The Collapse and Revival of American Community* (New York: Simon & Schuster, 2000).

Rahner, Karl, "The Sin of Adam," in *Theological Investigations*, trans. David Bourke (New York: Crossroad, 1982), 11:249–50.

Riesman, David, *The Lonely Crowd: A Study of the Changing American Character* (New Haven: Yale University Press, 2001).

Rothenberg, Paula S., *White Privilege: Essential Readings on the Other Side of Racism* (New York: Worth Publishers, 2002).

Seligman, Martin E. P., *Authentic Happiness: Using the New Positive Psychology to Realize Your Potential for Lasting Fulfillment* (New York: Atria Press, 2003).

Trible, Phyllis, "Eve and Adam: Genesis 2–3 Reread," *Andover Newton Quarterly* 13, no. 4 (March 1973): 251–58.

The Second Wall

Envy

You shall not covet your neighbor's house; you shall not covet your neighbor's wife, or male or female slave, or ox, or donkey, or anything that belongs to your neighbor.

— Exodus 20:17

THE GOOD ANOTHER HAD

A scene that took place one Christmas morning at my parents' house illustrates envy well. About twelve of their grandchildren were assembled there. Three of the boys were very young, between eighteen and twenty months old, and this was their first Christmas together. Everyone in the family was seated in front of a huge pile of presents, waiting for my father to come from his bedroom and sit in his chair: the signal that the opening of presents could begin. Twelve children tearing open their packages was like a feeding frenzy; it took all of ten minutes. The scene was pure pandemonium, with excited laughter, exclamations of gratitude, ringing bells, buzzing buzzers, and the beeping of electronic games.

My mother had gotten the three youngest boys the same present. Mitchell, Shane, and Patrick each had in front of him a red truck wrapped up in a gold box with a ribbon on top. While the older kids were making mayhem, the little boys were having fun just playing with the ribbons on their boxes. Finally someone noticed that the little boys had not opened their presents yet. Our attention and a couple of video cameras were trained on them, and everyone began urging the boys to open their gifts. After much coaching, Shane figured out how to open his package, and he found the one thing that he most dearly loved: a toy truck. He lifted it up like some ancient totem. The other two boys stopped opening their presents and stared, open-mouthed at Shane's red truck. When the other boys began to reach for the truck, Shane covered it with his body. My mother and sisters hurried to show the other boys that they had this exact same red truck. But Mitchell and Patrick did not want their red trucks; they wanted Shane's red truck. And so the ruckus began. The unhappiness took hours to resolve and decidedly disrupted the holiday celebration.

Even at their young age, the boys seemed programmed to desire the good that another had rather than enjoying the good that was already theirs. Envy, jealousy, and rivalry pervade human experience from the very beginning of life and work systematically to break communal bonds and tear apart the harmony of individuals and communities in a myriad of ways. Three miserable toddlers on Christmas morning clearly showed that any attempt to understand human happiness or desire for the good life must account for the effects of covetousness, as the scriptures call it, on human interactions in any culture.

Understanding Envy

In the Hebrew scripture's account of history, envy becomes the leitmotif of the human descent into sin and social chaos. Envy is actually the first sin noted in the Bible: Adam and Eve envy God because God has something they do not and God won't give it to them, even though they have all that they need and are otherwise perfectly content (Gen 3:2–7). To follow the history of covetousness: Cain envies Abel. Ten brothers envy Joseph. David covets Uriah's wife. The Israelites envy their neighbors' lives, properties, and religions. The Pharisees are jealous of Jesus. The older brother envies the prodigal son. The Hellenistic Christians are jealous of the Jewish Christians (Acts 6:1–7) and vice versa (Acts 14:48–52). There are many more examples. Stories of people wanting something that belongs to someone else fill both the Hebrew and Christian scriptures, which honestly recount the chaos that inevitably ensues.

The Ten Commandments (Ex 20:1–17; Deut 5:6–21) embody this understanding of covetousness as a principle source of evil in the world. Significantly, the tenth commandment is the longest commandment in the second part of the Decalogue: "You shall not covet your neighbor's house; you shall not covet your neighbor's wife, or male or female slave, or ox, or donkey, or anything that belongs to your neighbor" (Ex 20:17; cf. Deut 5:21). This commandment is fundamentally different from the preceding five; it prohibits covetousness itself, whereas the others prohibit the sins that often result from covetousness: murder, adultery, theft, bearing false witness. Although in the last and seemingly least position, the tenth commandment, in a way, summarizes the rest and indicates just what attitude is necessary to protect human relationships from the covetous desires and impulses. In and of itself, covetousness will wreck any bonds of commitment and mutual love and make genuine community impossible.

According to the Gospel narratives, both jealousy and envy were the reasons the religious and civil authorities persecuted and eventually executed Jesus of Nazareth. The various religious leaders that Jesus encountered envied his personal virtue and were jealous of the charismatic authority with average people that Jesus possessed. Jesus then baffled these authorities with his nonviolent and passive response to their conspiracy; and when he continued to speak truth to the rich and powerful, challenging their hypocritical claims to authority, he subverted their conventional worldview and frightened them at an existential, visceral level. They had to kill him because his very existence undermined everything they embraced as true.

Yet Jesus refused to hate them back or to resist them in any way. He would not collude with them by rallying his followers in a movement that would create more chaos and bloodshed. Instead, he forgave his persecutors and urged his disciples to do the same. In so doing, Jesus not only rejected the jealousy and rivalry that infected his culture, he also offered a way out of the mire and chaos that that these emotions create.

Jesus' response shows how one can redirect one's desires to God's original vision for creation. In imitation of God, Jesus chose to share his own life rather than taking or coveting what others possess (Mt 5). The incarnation itself, at least in Saint Paul's understanding, represents God's miraculous self-offering that subverts the dominant patterns of envy and rivalry and substitutes shared experience and enhanced bonds of generosity and friendship (see especially Rom 8:1–27; 12; 15:1–13). Paul and the Gospel writers taught that God's self-offering would continue beyond Jesus' presence on Earth through the gift of the divine Spirit (2 Cor 3:16–18). According to the Christian scriptures, this Spirit enlivens all that receive it, re-creating them in the image of Jesus Christ and drawing them into the beloved community to share God's gracious presence.[1]

What is envy? What fosters it? How does it influence human perception? Is it inevitable? The ancient great Greek philosopher Aristotle provided some insights. He believed that most human knowing comes through imitation, that the "instinct of imitation" is implanted in the human psyche from birth and is the means through which most lessons about life are learned.[2] Through imitation children learn how to speak, behave, and conduct almost all interpersonal and social functions. According to Aristotle, the ability to imitate enables humans to interpret the world, think rationally about it, and communicate with others through complex symbols (such as those used in stories, songs, and art).

Thomas Aquinas (1225–1274), influential Roman Catholic theologian and philosopher, accepted Aristotle's fundamental insight but viewed it through a Christian lens. According to Aquinas, as a result of original sin, all human instincts and desires, while fundamentally good, can be used for false or dangerous ends. Imitation followed inordinately can become envy, jealousy, and rivalry (*Summa Theologica* 1–2.84.1–2). In other words, people tend to distort their ability to learn through imitation into a powerful desire to take and posses other people's things (wealth, relationships, status, beauty,

---

1. For a thoughtful and readable explanation of the social and ethical dimensions of Paul's theology, see Jerome Murphy O'Connor, *Becoming Human Together: The Pastoral Anthropology of St. Paul* (Wilmington, DE: Michael Glazier, 1982).

2. This understanding of the epistemological function of imitation is dispersed throughout Aristotle's work, but his comments are most direct in *The Poetics*, 3.1: "Poetry in general seems to have sprung from two causes, each of them lying deep in our nature. First, the instinct of imitation is implanted in man from childhood, one difference between him and other animals being that he is the most imitative of living creatures, and through imitation learns his earliest lessons; and no less universal is the pleasure felt in things imitated. . . . Imitation, then, is one instinct of our nature."

knowledge, and so forth) as their own. In Aquinas's reasoning, this inordinate desire is the root cause of all other forms of human sinfulness and vice.

Further, Aquinas believed that envy would lead to the sin of pride. Pride is not merely an attitude of arrogance, superiority, or self-aggrandizement but, rather, "the inordinate desire to excel," a desire that manifests as extreme ambition, competitiveness, and the drive to better oneself "at any cost" (*Summa Theologica* 1-2.84.2).

Taken together, envy and pride become, for Aquinas, the "root and branch" of all human sinfulness.[3] All the other capital sins—lust, gluttony, sloth, greed, anger—arise from uncontrolled desire to have what others possess or to propel oneself above others without regard to their or any other greater good. He concluded that these disordered instincts, which drive people to believe that the diminishment of others is in their own best interest, cause most of the pain and suffering in the world.

Building upon Aquinas's analysis, contemporary literary critic and social theorist René Girard (1923–) contends that in addition to people's fundamental desire to imitate others, they come to desire what other people desire. He posits a human inability to perceive the world *except through* the eyes of others.[4] He calls this form of imitative activity "mimetic desire," meaning that not only do people desire what their neighbor's possess but also they learn to desire what others desire precisely because others desire it.[5] Mimetic desire leads to double idolatry in which people idolize both their neighbors and their neighbors' desires, and they also worship themselves

---

3. Here Aquinas is following the lead of scripture and actually trying to reconcile two seemingly conflicting accounts of the root of human sinfulness: Sirach 10:12–15, which posits that pride is the root of sin, and 1 Timothy 6:10, which claims that envy is its root.

4. René Girard develops his theory on mimetic desire and its effects in a number of works. Most notable are *Violence and the Sacred*, trans. Patrick Gregory (Baltimore: Johns Hopkins University Press, 1977); *Things Hidden Since the Foundation of the World* (New York: Continuum, 2003); and *I See Satan Fall Like Lightning* (Maryknoll, NY: Orbis Books, 2001). For an analysis of Girard's thought and its implications for theology, see James Allison, *Raising Abel: The Recovery of Eschatological Imagination* (New York: Crossroads, 1996). For a book that develops Girard's insights and connects them to the wider phenomenon of violence, see Gil Baile, *Violence Unveiled: Humanity at the ~ ~~roads* (New York Crossroads, 1997).

5. *Satan Fall Like Lightning*, 7–10.

by desperately trying to acquire the objects of the other's desire. This dual adulation creates rivalry at the heart of every social interaction, which easily erupts into conflict and finally violence. Left unchecked, it could lead to the breakdown of all kinds of human relationships and, ultimately, social chaos.

For this reason most societies would seek to limit the effects of mimetic desire by forbidding coveting and organizing shared social activities to symbolically deflect the conflict at the heart of human relationships. Different cultures have developed different religious activities or rituals for these purposes. One of these involves "scape-goating" a victim to appease the violent, often pent up, emotions of the community; this might even extend to actual sacrifice. Whatever the ritual might be, it breaks the cycle of mimetic rivalry and reestablishes relative harmony among individuals in the community.

While many cultures still maintain complex though subtle dimensions of this tendency as Girard explains, North American culture has strangely reinterpreted these ancient insights and converted these vices into virtues. In the logic of free-market capitalism, the inordinate desires to possess what others posses and to excel over others are understood not only as natural but also as fundamentally necessary for the "good" of the economy and, hence, of the society. Nowhere is this sentiment better portrayed than in the 1987 movie by Oliver Stone, *Wall Street*. In one of its most iconic scenes, the star Michael Douglas, playing the character Gordon Gekko, declares to an enthralled gathering of shareholders: "Greed, for lack of a better word, is good." Instead of restraining rivalry, free-market capitalism actually exploits it—with many of the chaotic and disastrous results that other societies have feared.

THE LOGIC OF THE MARKETPLACE

In *The Great Transformation*, his magnum opus on modern economic theory, historian and economist Karl Polanyi (1886–1964) describes the modern market economy as resting on the theory that self-regulating and self-adjusting markets, free from outside interference, are capable of meeting the demand for goods and services from the greatest number of people over time in the most efficient means possible—thus improving the overall quality of life of the whole society.[6] This belief in the power of self-regulating markets to improve the common good rests on two fundamental hypotheses: The first, an almost mystical belief, is that human progress is a universal inevitability; Polanyi calls this concept "mystical readiness." This belief is firmly rooted in the Enlightenment's sense of progress and specifically in the economic theories that emerged in the seventeenth and eighteenth centuries. The second hypothesis is that the underlying motive for most human judgments is to improve one's economic situation.

Adam Smith (1723–1790), philosopher, economist, and author of the immensely influential text *The Wealth of Nations* (1776), put forth this idea. He believed that humans had a natural "propensity to barter, truck, and exchange things for another."[7] This belief led him to assert that the most basic and predictable aspect of human nature was economic activity; thus was born the concept of the economic person, a being who acts primarily in his or her own best economic interests. According to the theory of the economic person, the political, intellectual, and spiritual dimensions of human life are always subservient to economic considerations. In sum, Polanyi proposes that market capitalism is rooted in the twin assumptions of spontaneous progress and economic imperatives.

Given capitalism's uncritical belief in continuously adjusting, self-regulating markets, all of a society's assets became commodities to be bought and sold at will. Before the rise of market economies, land, labor, and even money had intrinsic value—that is, value above and beyond their mere market value. They signified stable social relationship and human dignity. They were the common patrimony of the whole community and the just and obligatory means of distributing goods to all according to the needs of each. In a radically free-market economy, however, all of these traditional, and even sacred, assets could be assigned certain values and then be exchanged like all other commodities. The commodification of land, labor, and money signaled a seismic shift in the way that communities would function.

---

6. Karl Polanyi, *The Great Transformation: The Political and Economic Origins of Our Time* (Boston: Beacon Press, 1957), 35.

7. Adam Smith, *An Inquiry into the Nature and Cause of the Wealth of Nations*, ed. Edwin Cannan (New Rochelle, NY: Arlington House, 1966).

Polanyi, on the contrary, asserts that economic life never functioned autonomously from the broader social and cultural milieu with which it was interwoven. He believes that a community's economic life is always embedded in its social structures and creates a web of social relationships that need to be nurtured and maintained. When market capitalism insisted on "freeing" markets from traditional social restraints and obligations so as to answer only to the supply and demand for commodities, all dimensions of society—political, cultural, religious, and ethical—were subordinated to the market's needs and patterns. The institutionalization of free-market ideology created not just a new economic system but also eventually a new social system: the free-market economy morphed into a "free-market society" in which the "value" of everything depends on its market price.

As history has shown, societies have inevitably taken steps to protect themselves and limit the overwhelming impact of free markets on social relationship and individuals. The result has been a "double movement" in which each society has simultaneously attempted to advance laissez-faire markets while developing social mechanisms to limit the cultural damage that has inevitably resulted from laissez-faire economics.[8] Most Western societies, however, have never seemed to question the underlying economic ideology, and instead go to great lengths to maintain the illusion of the self-regulating market and to subordinate broader social needs to economic ones. For this reason, Polanyi insists that a self-regulating, self-adjusting market is a utopia based on specious assumptions and upheld at great costs to persons and society as whole—resting on presumptions that are not experientially verifiable and that cannot be achieved without great social costs. A free-market institution "could not exist for any length of time without annihilating the human and natural substance of society; it would have physically destroyed man and turned his surrounding into a wilderness."[9]

Despite the contrary evidence that Polanyi identifies, free-market societies remain intractable in promoting the centrality of free markets. This ideology has given rise to what Polanyi refers to as the "liberal

8. Polanyi, *The Great Transformation*, 138.
9. Ibid., 3.

creed": "a veritable faith in man's secular salvation through self-regulating markets."[10] Two nineteenth-century social theorists, Herbert Spencer and Charles Darwin, provided the "scientific" evidence for this creed: if humans are really just an advanced species of animal, they will predictably act in ways that ultimately foster the survival of the species. Thus even the basest human instincts and behaviors can be viewed as perfectly "natural" and necessary.

Given this understanding of reality, what were previously considered sins or aberrations of nature—such as envy, pride, ambition, and greed—are now just inherent and necessary aspects of human nature. Moreover, by using these strong human desires to advance the common good of the species, free markets became a form of grace, offering "salvation" from past dogmas that muted human nature and bound human potential in "unnatural" ways. In other words, envy and pride are natural instincts that enable humans to compete and survive in society and that lead to a higher good by unleashing the economic propensities that make humans unique among the other animals.

The United States has accepted the liberal creed almost unquestioningly as the foundation of economic policy and as the way to achieve the "good life" and the pursuit of happiness promised in the nation's Declaration of Independence. By implication, success becomes equated with happiness. To be successful is to receive the highest market price for whatever commodities one has to barter or sell and to use the proceeds to acquire whatever other commodities might be necessary to live a good life. This good life is only incidentally related to an ethical life; instead, the good is directly associated with personal happiness derived from pleasure, leisure, fulfillment of desire, and free self-expression. This market system works only because humans have an instinct to desire, and hence to acquire, what others desire or have acquired. Envy drives the free-market system, determining the relative value of each commodity and creating new markets and new commodities.[11]

---

10. Ibid., 141.

11. See more about the concept of commodity fetish in Marx, *Economic and Philosophical Manuscripts of 1844: The Marx-Engels Reader*, ed. Robert C. Tucker (New York: Norton, 1972). See also Vincent J. Miller, *Consuming Religion: Christian Faith and Practice in a Consumer Culture* (New York: Continuum, 2004), 36–39.

Mimetic desire can be seen as the foundation of the free-market economy. The fields of advertising and marketing are focused on getting people to desire more commodities precisely because other people desire them, and because these commodities are desirable, their possession is a sure sign of success.

THE CHRISTIAN CREED
AND THE LIBERAL CREED

One would expect that religion, and especially Christianity, would provide a much-needed critique of and antidote to the free-market ideology. However, in a free-market society, religion itself becomes a commodity of the marketplace.[12] As a commodity, religion adjusts itself to meet the demands of the market, becoming the kind of therapeutic religion discussed earlier that does not question the common sense of the society in which it is embedded. In his invaluable analysis in *Protestantism and the Rise of Western Capitalism*, Max Weber attempts to demonstrate that capitalism and Calvinistic Protestantism became mutually interdependent on one another in the early stages of modernity.[13] Protestantism created both a work ethic and a simple lifestyle that over time led to a large accumulation of wealth by those who were most religiously devout. Eventually, Weber maintains, expanding wealth became identified with a sanctified state, while poverty connoted moral and spiritual degradation. As theologian Kathryn Tanner points out, money was substituted for grace, and one became the sign of the other.[14] Although it has fallen into some disfavor, Weber's study nevertheless shows the important intersection between the Calvinistic religious tradition on which the United States was founded and the free-market capitalism that quickly took hold in the American ethos.

Americans, many of whom are rooted in some version of this strain of Calvinism, have easily embraced the idea that self-regulating

---

12. For an analysis of this trend, see Miller, *Consuming Religion*, especially 73–106.

13. Max Weber, *The Protestant Ethic and the Spirit of Capitalism*, trans. Talcott Parsons (New York: Scribners, 1958).

14. Kathryn Tanner, *Economy of Grace* (Minneapolis MN: Augsburg Fortress, 2005), 6–8.

free markets will inevitably lead to the greatest good. The Calvinist settlers believed that God controls human destiny completely, such that nothing an individual might do can affect one's ultimate end. Given the economic prosperity of the Calvinist communities, it was easy for them to substitute the free market for God. By conflating sin and nature Calvinism often unwittingly endorsed the anthropology of liberal capitalism, which made inordinate human instincts to be natural desires that inevitably have to be pursued. The notion of self-regulating free markets and the mystical faith in progress serve as secular versions of the Calvinist concepts of Providence: both believe that mystical but necessary forces control human destiny in a way that makes humans almost impotent to affect the social order. Humans simply live out a largely predetermined pattern of activity that is either divinely or naturally orchestrated so that salvation is assured.

With the exception of religious communities that explicitly advocate an alternative lifestyle (such as various Mennonite, Amish, or other Anabaptist groups or perhaps some cloistered monastics), Christianity seems oddly unaware of its complicity in the dominant culture's shifting views of the value of human life. Despite the Judeo-Christian scriptures' numerous admonitions to lift up society's outcasts, particularly the impoverished, many US Christians seem unconcerned about the presence of deep-rooted economic injustice in the United States.

The role of the Roman Catholic Church in the United States is quite complex. Catholicism was essentially an immigrant church throughout the nineteenth and early twentieth centuries. Its close ties to immigrants led it to become a fierce advocate of unions and other social mechanisms that limited the effects of the market economy on the poor and the working class. Furthermore, the late nineteenth-century papacy's rejection of new models of political, social, scientific, and economic advancements (often referred to by the Church as modernism) included strong critiques of both expressions of the liberal creed: free-market capitalism and what the church called collectivism (that is, communism). Beginning with the papal encyclical *Rerum novarum* (On the Condition of Labor, 1891), the Catholic Church's social teachings proclaimed that all social and economic systems had to be based on the "truth" of the fundamental dignity of every human person, the indispensability of social relations, and the demands of justice that recognize the "other" as genuinely human and created to live according to a higher good.[15] In sum, the Catholic Church taught that humans and their relationships could not be solely defined by or reduced to their utility, contractual obligations, or private ownership.

This tradition of social teaching continued to develop and became especially prominent during the papacy of John Paul II. He issued a series of encyclicals that dealt with social issues and specifically challenged the dominance of the free market.[16] In 1986, the US bishops followed suit, specifically addressing the issues of economic policy, justice, and the economic common good in a pastoral letter titled *Economic Justice for All*.[17] Therein the bishops asserted, "basic justice demands the establishment of minimum levels of participation in the life of the human community for all persons."[18] In sum, every person has the fundamental right to life, work, clothing, shelter, rest, medical care, and education, and society as a whole has an obligation to secure these rights. As basic elements of human dignity, these fundamentals are not open to the fluctuations or contingencies of the free market. Both the bishops and the pope insisted that the market system be modified in such a way that "the needs of the poor take priority over the desires of the rich; the rights of workers over the maximization of profits; the preservation of the environment over uncontrolled industrial expansion; production to meet social needs over production for military purposes."[19] While it is not clear that this strong tradition of social teaching greatly influenced the opinions of the majority US Catholics, it remains a prominent critique of unrestrained liberal capitalism.[20]

---

15. See *The Compendium of the Social Doctrine of the Church* (Washington, DC: USCCB, 2005), 87–90.

16. See especially the *Compendium of the Social Doctrine of the Church*, for the best compilation and explanation of official Catholic social teaching.

17. *Economic Justice for All: Pastoral Letter on Catholic Social Teaching and the U.S. Economy* (Washington, DC: USCCB, 1997).

18. Ibid., no. 77.

19. Ibid., no. 94, from an address that John Paul II made in Canada in 1984.

20. Robert Bellah, et al. *The Good Society* (New York: Alfred A. Knopf, 1991), 106, 248; Robert Lekachman, *Visons and Nightmares: America after Reagan* (New York: Macmillan, 1987), 227–32.

AN AMERICAN TRAGEDY

Greek tragedies are usually characterized by the reversal of fortune of a great person who is brought down either because of a character flaw or a conflict with some higher power such as the gods, fate, society, or the law. In *Poetics,* Aristotle defined the tragic archetype as "that of a man who is not eminently good and just yet whose misfortune is brought about not by vice or depravity but also by some error or frailty. He must be one who is highly renowned and prosperous—a personage such as Oedipus, Thyestes, or other illustrious men of such families."[21] Greek tragedy was organized around three main actions: the complication, the unraveling, and the "catharsis." Catharsis is the effect of either viewing or participating in the drama in such a way that one's own frailty, character flaws, or deeper conflicts are exposed, appreciated, and ultimately diminished. Girard and others have outlined how this dramatic structure mainstreamed the religious process of ritual sacrifice and purification, achieving for the civic community the same benefit that the religious community had enjoyed. In Girard's words, the sacrifice of a victim in the dramatic story serves to "purge the spectators of their [individual and collective] passions and provoke a new katharsis, . . . [which] will restore the health and well-being of the community."[22] A Greek tragedy intentionally evokes pity, sympathy, and sorrow in the audience, thereby modifying and disempowering the negative urges and passions of the community: the drama provides a kind of release through the vicarious experience of the event.

Now jump several millennia forward. In 1907, American novelist Theodore Dreiser (1871–1945) writes about what he considered to be a particularly American crime: an ambitious young man's murder of the woman he loves because she stands in the way of his marriage to a woman of a higher class.[23] In the story that Dreiser intended to tell, the ambitious young man would have been a praiseworthy hero for achieving such a high social standing were it not for the unfortunate killing. Unlike the ancient Greek plays, the great American

---

21. *Poetics,* 2.13.

22. Girard, *Violence and the Sacred,* 290.

23. Theodore Dreiser, *An American Tragedy,* with new introduction by Richard Lingeman (New York: Penguin Group, 2000), viii.

drama depicted ordinary people rising out of poverty into prosperity through personal determination and hard work.[24] Dreiser felt that a murder such as he envisioned would constitute a profound American tragedy. He realized the insidious effects of envy and ambition in a nation in which economic success and access to the upper-class lifestyle were considered the pinnacle of the American dream.

Dreiser knew that the American dream had the potential to become a nightmare in a culture that made base human desires the bedrock of normal, moral, and even "wise" human actions. In a society in which the majority are economic outsiders who want to be insiders, many narratives revolve around the outsider who penetrates the boundaries of economic and class exclusion and enters into fullness of American life. However, those unable to traverse the social barriers despite their hard work and ambition often endure tragic consequences. Dreiser's particularly American tragedy requires neither a character flaw nor human frailty or higher powers to destroy the main character. In fact, the character's absolute and unwavering adherence to the highest values of his society proves his undoing. Success itself in a misguided and flawed social context can lead to violence, sorrow, and despair.

In 1925, Dreiser's project came to fruition in *An American Tragedy*. Based on an actual event, it is the story of Clyde Griffiths, who begins his life in almost complete poverty and social isolation as the son of religious social workers and traveling preachers.

Clyde grows up and eventually discovers and allies himself with a distant uncle who has made a small fortune running a clothing factory. There he meets and eventually falls in love with Roberta, a lower-class working girl. When Roberta becomes pregnant, she insists that Clyde marry her. Clyde, however, has become involved with Sondra, a wealthy and well-connected friend of his relatives. Once Clyde glimpses the economic and social possibilities that Sondra might be able to provide, even his genuine love for Roberta cannot stand against his desire to join the wealthy class. Because Roberta and his unborn child are obstacles to his prosperity and success, he shrewdly takes Roberta out rowing into the middle of a lake with the

---

24. David Brooks, an op-ed writer for the *New York Times*, makes a similar observation in his column on September 20, 2003. Brooks cites the work of Saul Bellow as an example of this twentieth-century version of the American "epic."

intention of murdering her. Circumstances strangely go awry, but he allows her to drown when the boat overturns—sad about the accident but ultimately remorseless about the fatality.

The narrative then turns to Clyde's trial for murder, conviction, and execution. This judicial process ultimately exposes the hypocrisy of the social system that both Roberta and Clyde so fervently desired to join. His execution serves as a catharsis, a wiping away of the stain of his sin and the indictment of the whole social system it represents. In essence, this catharsis, to put it in Girard's terms, relieves the conscience of those who are complicit with Clyde in his steadfast belief that getting ahead at any cost is a valid force in American life. Yet, the question is left unanswered: was Clyde's sin that he broke acceptable boundaries to get ahead or that he simply got caught doing so? Neither Clyde nor any other person in the narrative ever repents or even fully acknowledges the real sin—that of boundless envy and ambition. In fact, Clyde's execution is necessary to forestall a more penetrating introspection into the very foundations of the American dream.

Understanding that the "heroic" attempt to rise out of poverty can have tragic consequences, Dreiser also portrays the profound role that class distinctions play in American culture. These privileges both fuel envy and are the fruit of it. In theory, on the market playing field, the winners secure the American dream and attain the good life. However, the misfortunes and sorrows of the losers are not solely personal and, in fact, set in motion unintended consequences that imperil the good life and the American dream for everyone.

THE JONESES' PROBLEM

In modern American culture, this collision of envy, ambition, class, and marketplace logic has become popularly known as keeping up with the Joneses. As the term implies, a need to keep up or move ahead of one's neighbors can deeply color American social life. While this outlook generates upward mobility for some, those who are left out of the economic process experience anger, frustration, and despair. The exclusion is systemic: whole parts of the populations are unable to participate. This exclusion can in turn lead to increasing class, racial, and cultural tensions: because advertising invades every dimension of American life, even people at the lowest end of economic well-being are bombarded with scenes of the good life, an American dream to which they have no real access.[25] The forces of the marketplace do not allow everyone to participate in the material wealth and lifestyle that is sold to them on a daily basis. Some people turn to violence to express their frustrations, to crime to seize a small portion of what the media shows them they should have, or to drug and alcohol abuse in response to the inequalities and injustices they cannot escape. In other words, Clyde Griffith's fear that he would somehow be left out of the American dream has become generalized in American society.

In *Washington City Paper*, Joe Lapp has written about his personal story as the son of an Amish-Mennonite minister who grew up in the inner-city housing projects of Washington, DC, and returned to continue his father's work to build peaceful relationships across social and racial barriers.[26] Titled, "Thou Shalt Not Covet Thy Neighbor's Dodge Minivan," his article insists that the differences in and degrees of class have changed dramatically since his childhood in the late 1950s and early 1960s. He also observes an exponential increase in the level of violence, much of it simply reckless, aimless. What Lapp narrates is largely the story of people who in one generation went from being poor and economically dispossessed to being systematically and structurally excluded from what they consider ordinary and even necessary material blessings. In Lapp's analysis, this exclusion fuels a burning rage, largely unfocused but with roots in what Lapp perceives as the kind of coveting that is socially ingrained in many in America from a very early age.

Changes in criminal activity among the structurally poor are not without consequences for those who have supposedly achieved the American dream. The violence is not only "poor on poor" but also spills over into the communities of those who are economically better off. Within the world of the middle and upper classes, the prevalence of guns and other weapons for defense against crime leads to higher and more violent crimes within these

---

25. For a classic analysis of this cycle, see Robert Lekachman, *Visons and Nightmares* (New York: Macmillan, 1987), 265–76.

26. Joe Lapp, "Thou Shalt Not Covet Thy Neighbor's Dodge Minivan," *Washington City Paper* 26, no. 46 (November 17–22, 2006): 17–22.

classes.[27] However, the fear of crime for the upper classes far out-weighs its reality, imprisoning the wealthy in their communities while driving them to restrict the poor even further. Instead of help-ing their brothers and sisters, the "Moses figures" in America—those who are living the good life in "pharaoh's house"—simply turn their backs. It is a spiral of violence that is not well understood.

The extravagant expansion of wealth in the United States but the narrowness with which it has been distributed have far deeper repercussions than just class conflicts. When the Joneses them-selves cannot keep up with their peers—as the *New York Times* has reported, the very rich are leaving the "merely rich" behind—even some well-to-do communities and professions feel extreme anxiety about falling behind.[28] There is a mounting gap not just of lifestyle but also of personal self-interpretation and meaning because every-one in the society expects to better himself or herself and even needs to in order to have some sense of self-worth.[29]

In the logic of free-market capitalism it makes sense to con-stantly strive for something more. It is logical to not be content and happy as long as one sees others doing better than one's self. However, this kind of logic takes a great toll on good will. It creates class antagonisms and suspicion of immigrants and often a general resentment of anyone who is actually achieving the American dream. Rather than rejoicing in the inclusion of more and more people in the economic prosperity of the nation, many Americans respond selfishly and negatively to any proposed redistribution of wealth. The political landscape becomes more reactionary and polarized, and the social landscape turns into a playing board with too much emphasis on winning, sometimes at any cost.

In the biblical story, Moses eventually foregoes his status at pha-raoh's court and embraces the cause of his oppressed brethren—but

---

27. A good illustration of this phenomenon is Michael Moore's 2002 documentary *Bowling for Columbine*, in which he shows the dramatic differences between gun vio-lence in the United States and many other countries, including Canada, that have the same level of ownership of firearms but not nearly the level of violence from guns that Americans accept as normal.

28. Louis Uchitelle, "Very Rich Leaving the Merely Rich Behind," *New York Times*, November 27, 2006, 1, 18.

29. See further Christopher Lasch, *The Culture of Narcissism* (New York: Norton and Company, 1979).

it is possible to imagine a very different story unfolding. What if Moses, instead of developing a strong sense of empathy and compassion for others, had grown up feeling both increasingly entitled and yet victimized by his "unfair" association with the lower-class, socially outcast Hebrews? What if Moses, enjoying the luxury of being a member of pharaoh's house, began to feel that he wasn't receiving his fair share of status? What if Moses developed a deep resentment toward the Hebrew people and came to detest them as somehow depriving him of the fullness of respect and attainment of riches to which he felt he was entitled? Perhaps the story of Moses could have ended another way. Perhaps Moses could have used his power and influence to deprive the Hebrew people of even more dignity and rights; perhaps he could have even helped to rid the kingdom of them completely as a way of freeing himself and his adoptive people of their dangerous presence.

CONCLUSION

The Hebrew and Christian scriptures posit that envy or coveting lies at the heart of the social sinfulness that so greatly afflicts humanity. Both ancient sources and contemporary writers locate the source of human envy in the fundamental tendency to learn about the world, interpret reality, and make judgments through imitating other humans. The contemporary literary critic and social theorist René Girard names this process of knowing through imitation *mimetic desire*. Girard contends that while mimetic desire connotes a natural human tendency that can serve to aid societies in working together as cohesive social units, left unchecked, it can also lead to severe forms of social disruption and even violence. It is for this reason that the Hebrew and Christian traditions so greatly eschew envy and categorize it as the vice at the root of many other vices and sinful cycles of human activity.

The emergence of liberal capitalism and its almost mystical belief in self-regulating free markets rested simultaneously on the belief that human tendencies such as envy and greed actually served the common good of societies by denoting predictable human habits that would naturally balance one another and self-regulate the commercial and economic life of societies. The economist and historian Karl Polanyi described this vision of human nature and self-regulating markets as utopic and tried to demonstrate the inherent danger in uncritically accepting what he called the Liberal Creed of free-market capitalism. Polanyi spent his career trying to convince people that the naive belief in the Liberal Creed and the human propensity for envy and greed that underlays it, were inadequate to explain the ways that markets and economies really work and fundamentally dangerous to societies that embrace them. The Judeo-Christian ethical traditions were often skeptical about the Liberal Creed and unregulated free-market capitalism. Nevertheless, these same religious traditions also unwittingly endorsed the more fundamental anthropology that grounded these utopic ideologies.

In the US context the Liberal Creed lies at the heart of the cultural and social ethos in way that actually transformed the ancient vices of envy and greed into virtues. Rather than challenging and tempering envy as a dangerous human tendency, US culture accepted envy as a valid expression of individual and personal striving for success and self-fulfillment. This fundamental shift has had a number of negative consequences for US social life and continues to profoundly impact the experience of almost everyone who is exposed to the US social ethos. While it does not have tragic consequences for everyone, it does represent an "original sin" at the heart of American life that needs to be challenged by authentically converted Christians.

QUESTIONS FOR REFLECTION

1. Do the religious traditions you are familiar with view envy or covetousness as a vice or problem? How do you view it?

2. Do you find the Judeo-Christian traditional understanding of envy as described in this chapter persuasive? Why or why not?

3. What is your level of confidence in the free-market system? Do you consider it to be a utopic ideology that needs to be critically challenged by religious traditions? Why or why not?

4. Is the summary of Polanyi's critique offered in this chapter compelling? Why or why not?

5. To what extent are Christianity and free-market capitalism in conflict?

6. Assess the effect of envy on US social life. Is it a real problem? Why or why not?

FOR FURTHER READING

Allison, James, *Raising Abel: The Recovery of Eschatological Imagination* (New York: Crossroads, 1996).

Baile, Gil, *Violence Unveiled: Humanity at the Crossroads* (New York Crossroads, 1997).

The Compendium of the Social Doctrine of the Church (Washington, DC: USCCB, 2005).

Girard, René, *I See Satan Fall Like Lightning* (Maryknoll, NY: Orbis Books, 2001).

———. *Things Hidden Since the Foundation of the World* (New York: Continuum, 2003).

———. *Violence and the Sacred*, trans. Patrick Gregory (Baltimore: Johns Hopkins University Press, 1977).

Economic Justice for All: Pastoral Letter on Catholic Social Teaching and the U.S. Economy (Washington, DC: USCCB, 1997).

Hyde, Lewis, *The Gift: Imagination and the Erotic Life of Property*, First Vintage Books Edition (New York: Random House, 1979).

Kavanaugh, John F., *Following Christ in a Consumer Society: The Spirituality of Cultural Resistance* (Maryknoll, NY: Orbis Books, 1981).

Knitter, Paul F. and Chandra Muzaffat, eds., *Subverting Greed: Religious Perspectives on the Global Economy* (Maryknoll, NY: Orbis Press, 2002).

Miller, Vincent J., *Consuming Religion: Christian Faith and Practice in a Consumer Culture* (New York: Continuum, 2004).

Polanyi, Karl, *The Great Transformation: The Political and Economic Origins of Our Time* (Boston: Beacon Press, 1957), 35.

Smith, Adam, *An Inquiry into the Nature and Cause of the Wealth of Nations*, ed. Edwin Cannan (New Rochelle, NY: Arlington House, 1966).

Tanner, Kathryn, *Economy of Grace* (Minneapolis, MN: Augsburg Fortress, 2005).

The Third Wall

Superficial Optimism

You love life, but we love death. — OSAMA BIN LADEN

THE PROBLEM OF EVIL

One of the classic conundrums of Christian theology is the problem of evil. Briefly stated, the problem is this: if God is truly good and truly in charge of everything (i.e., omnipotent), why do bad things happen, even to good people? Why, indeed, does evil exist at all? For many people, the problem of evil leads to an even more basic question: does God exist? If one cannot arrive at a satisfying answer to the problem of evil, one is likely to conclude that the reason evil exists in the world is because there is no God or at least not the kind of God that Christians have traditionally believed in. Thus it is impossible to argue the case for the existence of the Christian God without also addressing the problem of evil.

Western culture's answers to the question of evil have tended to imply that God is deficient in some area of divine capability. Science would contend, for instance, that if God exists, God would have to be morally neutral, creating and maintaining the universe according to laws and tendencies over which God cannot or does not interfere. Other apologists for God's inaction in the face of overwhelming evil would generally assert that God is not omnipotent in the classic sense; God is deeply sympathetic to our human plight but does not have the power to actually change our situation except through an intervention into human consciousness that gives strength and courage in the face of evil. Some would even argue that God does not fully comprehend the scope of human misery because God too is caught up in the processes of universal history that are still unfolding. So the Western response to the problem of evil is in some ways to accept serious limitations on God's desire or power to do anything about the crisis of human suffering and their tendency for global destruction.

While it is true that more than 90 percent of Americans believe in God or some higher power, doubts stemming precisely from the limitations humans place on the Deity seriously diminish this belief.[1] Such doubts instill in people, often subconsciously, a fear that there is no divine power at the heart of the universe in which one can trust or upon which one can depend. These contradictions of belief and unbelief, of trust and fear, go unchallenged as long as life remains stable and coherent. When chance events, suffering, loss, misery, sorrow, or any of the many manifestations of evil in human life upend this stability, people are thrown back on a belief system that cannot sufficiently account for just such events. In many respects, American life seems to be based on a presumption that is finally inconsistent with the realities of human history—a presumption that life is coherent and predictable, that the good life is available despite the pervasiveness of indiscriminate suffering, loss, and death.

On the morning of September 11, 2001, the uncritical presumption of many in the United States collided with the ideology of jihadist extremism.[2] This historical moment represented more than an abstract challenge to accepted religious beliefs: it struck much more surely at the fundamental contradiction at the core of American life.

---

1. See further "Global Index of Religion and Atheism" (WIN-Gallup International, 2012); "American Piety in the 21st Century: New Insights into the Depth and Complexity of Religion in the US," Baylor Religious Survey (Baylor University: Baylor Institute for Studies of Religion, 2006). See also Gallup News Service, "Values and Beliefs—Final Topline," Gallup Poll Social Series (Timberline: 927914, G: 788, Princeton Job #: 11-05-009; Jeff Jones, Lydia Saad), May 5–8, 2011; the website for the Pew Forum on Religion and Public Life at *www.pewform.org.*

2. See further Gilles Kepel and Peter Clark, "The Origins and Development of the Jihadist Movement: From Anti-Communism to Terrorism," *Asian Affairs* 34, no. 2 (July 2003): 91–109; Farhana Ali and Jerrold Post, "The History and Evolution of Martyrdom in Defensive Jihad: An Analysis of Suicide Bombers in Current Conflicts," *Social Research* 75, no. 2 (Summer 2008): 615–54; and Thomas Rid and Marc Hecker, "The Terror Fringe," *Policy Review* 158 (December 2009/January 2010), 3–19.

Jihadist extremism, rooted in a very narrow and modern inter-pretation of Islam (a type of pseudo-Islamic ideology), contains ele-ments of truth and contradiction—much like the American ideology discussed in the previous chapters. Pseudo-Islamic fundamentalism is also similar to American ideology in that it possesses the power to sustain people over a long period.

A more troubling similarity lies at the center of both ideolo-gies. Adherents of both justify participation in widespread and seem-ingly meaningless destruction through religious and pseudo-religious beliefs in their own divine destiny. That a group of pseudo-Islamic terrorists would carry out such a vicious attack on a civilian office complex was heinous, but what about the American response? Given that the Al-Qaeda bases that planned 9/11 were located in Afghan-istan, some would argue that the American invasion of that country was justified, but what about the much larger and bloodier invasion of Iraq that followed—a country that even at the time was acknowl-edged not to have been involved in the 9/11 attacks?

Apparently Americans, as a group, are willing to assume that all unfriendly Islamic dictatorships or countries are potential enemies that must be fought. More fundamentally, Americans, as a group, believe that the United States should extend the ideals and processes of American culture to the predominantly Islamic people of the Middle East. The pseudo-Islamic terrorists, in turn, believe that it is necessary to prevent the United States from extending its control and spreading the American way of life throughout the Middle East. More fundamentally, they believe that non-Muslims are infidels to be put to death and that the ideals and processes of Islamic culture should be spread to the non-Muslim people worldwide.

The mastermind of the 9/11 attack, Osama bin Laden, char-acterized the struggle between these two cultural ideologies with his statement, "You love life, but we love death." Clearly, his words indicate the significance of death in pseudo-Islamic fundamentalism and its relationship to violence against what it perceives as cultural aggressors. Such an embrace of death would say a great deal about how the impoverished and oppressed people of the Middle East and Southeast Asia interpret their lives if bin Laden were speaking for the majority, but he wasn't. One must also acknowledge the accuracy of bin Laden's insight into American life. As previously discussed,

Americans claim the "love of life" as a founding principle and pursue life—particularly what is termed the good life—with unrestrained personal and social zeal. The pursuit of happiness has become an end in itself to which all other endeavors must defer. When the American invasion of Iraq is justified as a means of defending the US way of life, the internal ideology of many in the United States becomes overt bellicosity.

OPTIMISM VERSUS HOPE

Americans are generally positive and optimistic about this life and its potential for enjoyment and happiness. At the same time, many Americans lack confidence about the future and rarely have any substantial vision for the years to come. Practically speaking, this lack of vision leads people to a kind of nihilistic materialism that causes them to get what they can while they can. It's often expressed, semi-jokingly, as "the one who dies with the most toys wins." Physicist and theologian J. C. Polkinghorne labels this sentiment the "tyranny of the present" for it is based on the fear that opportunities must be immediately attained or they will pass away forever.[3] Many in the United States are willing to sacrifice a great deal for the sake of personal achievement and material success in the present but are less willing to forgo present opportunities for future possibilities. Placing little value on the future, they live for today in ways that not only preclude making choices for the future but also result in regret for missed opportunities. Many people mourn the lives they did not lead.

Optimism requires a positive attitude and a commitment to change for the better in the face of adversity. However, it also requires living in a stable, secure society in which the ordinary necessities of life (food, clothing, housing, education) are available to everyone. When life is difficult, a positive attitude is much more difficult to sustain.

Optimism without stability and security is foolish, and those in the United States took a hit when the World Trade Center collapsed.

---

3. J. C. Polkinghorne, *The God of Hope and the End of the World* (New Haven: Yale University Press, 2002), 49.

The United States reacted violently out of terror that some impoverished and nearly powerless people half a world away might take away the good life. To regain even a false sense of security, US citizens allowed the president to limit personal freedoms with the Patriot Act, invade foreign countries, empower military tribunals, and so desecrate the very ideals they supposedly hold most dear. However, perhaps American ideals are not as dear as the American pursuit of happiness. Is there some truth in the pseudo-Islamic fundamentalist characterization of Americans as self-centered, individualistic, hedonistic, and morally bankrupt?

Why were Americans so terrorized by an event that, while horrible and audacious, was by no means a genuine threat to the life and stability of the nation? The terrorist leader, bin Laden, succinctly expressed the reason. He well understood that a love of the present life arises from a lack of hope in the future. Americans tend not to distinguish between optimism and hope. The idea that everything will be all right if people work hard with good intentions captures American optimism. Hope, however, is an understanding that present suffering will eventually give way to future happiness, that the earthly quest reaches its destination in a future reward. Optimism is based on the way things are supposed to be and holds the individual responsible for his or her own fulfillment. Hope places itself in the care of a higher power (or God) that can deliver on a promise for the future. In the decade since 9/11, Americans may have recovered some of their optimism about life and its possibilities, but at another level they have less and less hope in the ultimate outcome of their endeavors. This lack of hope walls in people—it traps them in a web of fear that they often cannot see beyond. Ultimately, mere optimism is powerless to overcome and enable people to see beyond the walls that fear and hopelessness create.

As Polkinghorne points out, even those with a theological background tend to confuse hope with optimism and common wishful thinking. Many priests and ministers often refer to hope not as a virtue to be cultivated but as an emotional feeling to be manipulated. Quoting Janet Soskice, a fellow theologian, he observes that "in the churches today there is a tendency to represent hope as if it were a psychological mood. 'Lack of faith and charity can be treated by prayer, but the lack of hope is treated with antidepressants.'"[4] For Christians, this approach represents a pastoral disaster.

Hope always points to a future beyond the scope of mere individual lives, but it is not passive. Polkinghorne insists on the necessary connection between hope and action. Because hope is not simply a mood one has but a vision in which one firmly believes, it moves those who have it to present action. As he asserts, "we should hope for what we are prepared to work for and to bring about, as far as that power lies within us."[5]

This strange contradiction between prevailing optimism and widespread lack of hope is not a brand new phenomenon in the United States. More than fifty years ago, Martin Luther King Jr. observed a great dearth of hope arising from a fear of change and a terror of death. He believed this deprivation caused a kind of moral paralysis that permitted inaction in the face of obvious injustice, a fatalistic acceptance of the "way things are" because things would just naturally "turn out alright." However, mere optimism about the way things would turn out was unacceptable in the face of racial hatred, vast poverty, and nuclear war. In numerous speeches and sermons, King called people to move away from superficial optimism and to embrace the vitality of authentic hope. In his book *Strength to Love* he described the reality of hope and its potential as follows:

> The answer lies in our willing acceptance of unwanted and unfortunate circumstances even as we cling to a radiant hope, our acceptance of finite disappointment even as we adhere to infinite hope. This is not the grim, bitter acceptance of the fatalist . . . [nor is it] to follow the escapist method of attempting to put the disappointment out of your mind which will lead to psychologically injurious repression. Place your failure at the forefront of your mind and stare daringly at it. Ask yourself, "How may I transform this liability into an asset? How may I, confined in some narrow Roman cell and unable to reach life's

---

4. J. C. Polkinghorne, *The God of Hope*, 47; he is quoting J. M. Soskice, in *The End of the World and the Ends of God*, ed. J. C. Polkinghorne and M. Welker (London: Trinity International Press, 2000), 78.

5. Polkinghorne, *The God of Hope*, 47–48.

Spain,[6] transmute this dungeon of shame into a haven of redemptive suffering?" Almost anything that happens to us may be woven into purposes of God. It may lengthen our cords of sympathy. It may break our self-centered pride. The cross, which was willed by wicked men, was woven by God into the tapestry of the world's redemption.[7]

King's understanding of hope was rooted primarily in the Christian scriptures and especially in the visionary rhetoric of Saint Paul. For both Paul and King, hope ultimately finds its source in the unique potential of God to control and transform history. That God has a plan for the universe and the power to carry it out lies at the heart of Christian hope. Hope is hope in God. Beyond a simplistic optimism that blindly wishes for something good, hope depends on a vision of a future that will vanquish even the most terrible realities of human history.

When Americans imagine a future life, they tend toward murky, abstract ideas that they pull together as a concept of heaven. The vision is pleasant enough—a happy and peaceful next life for one's soul—but it is often superficial and venial and functions more as a psychological fantasy than a concrete expectation of what the future holds for the individual and the world as a whole. The typical American image of heaven doesn't provide the support people need when real crises arise. In times of deep trouble or loss, believers who hold superficial visions of heaven will despair because they don't trust God's power and the future that God promises.

In their study, *Heaven: A History*, Colleen McDannell and Bernhard Lang conclude with a report on the notion of heaven in contemporary Western Christianity: "Life after death for many Christians, means existing only in the memory of their families and God. Scientific, philosophical and theological skepticism has nullified heaven and replaced it with teachings that are minimalist, meager, and dry."[8]

---

6. A reference to Acts 25–28 about Paul's imprisonment and journey to Rome where he hopes to continue proclaiming the gospel to the Romans and on to the ends of the empire.

7. Martin Luther King Jr., *Strength to Love* (New York: Harper and Row, 1963), 100.

8. Colleen McDannell and Bernhard Lang, *Heaven: A History* (New Haven: Yale University Press, 1988), 352.

Heaven understood so vaguely is often insufficient to strengthen and encourage people facing suffering and death.

The belief in life causes Americans—even Christian Americans—to fear death and deny the possibility that anything of value awaits them in death. This is not to say that they should swing to the other extreme, professing a belief in death that precludes and diminishes the goodness of this life. The way forward lies somewhere between these poles.

A DISCONNECTED DREAM

The dearth of hope in the presence of so much optimism is quite an obstacle to the achievement of happiness and peace—or the good life as deified in American culture. This irony has not been lost on the artists, poets, and writers of the last century. In the words of author Walker Percy,

> The poets and artists and novelists were saying something else: that at a time, when according to the theory of the age, men should feel most at home they felt most homeless. . . . In an age when communication theory and technique reached its peak, poets and artists were saying that men were in fact isolated and no longer communicated with each other. In the very age when the largest number of people lived together in the cities, poets and artists were saying that there no longer was a community. In the very age when men lived longest and were most secure in their lives, poets and artists were saying that men were most afraid. In the very age when crowds were largest and people flocked closest together, poets and artists were saying that men were lonely.[9]

Percy contends in his book *Message in a Bottle* that the traditional worldview no longer works, even when dressed up in the "attic finery of Judeo-Christianity."[10] Noting a profound disconnect between

---

9. Walker Percy, *The Message in the Bottle* (New York: Farrar, Strauss, and Giroux, 2000), 25.

10. Ibid., 21.

what people profess to believe and the realities of twentieth-century life, he asserts that the theories of the modern age are too abstract and unable to help people understand their lives in a coherent way.

Percy's insights imply that the absence of a viable understanding of the self has led to a decline in connectedness, community, and security in America. This lack of self-understanding can, in turn, be attributed to the loss of any utopia that ordinary people might use as a lens to interpret and appreciate their lives.

Perhaps more directly than anyone else, the Beat writers were able to express these losses and absences in ways that still resonate. The Beat Movement emerged in post–World War II San Francisco and New York. Although postwar America was experiencing an unprecedented period of prosperity and population growth, the Beat poets and artists tapped into an underlying restlessness and unhappiness, an almost inarticulate and persistent feeling that something was terribly wrong with the American dream.[11] American ideology was fraying on the edges, and its claims about the sources of human happiness were fraudulent. The disillusionment was strongest among young adults and was directed toward the monolithic, social middle-class ethos of white, Protestant America. Writers such as Jack Kerouac and William Burroughs and poets such as Allen Ginsberg, Kenneth Rexroth, Lawrence Ferlinghetti, and William Everson bared the cultural wasteland and social hypocrisy of American prosperity. Their work, while startling and unsettling to the broader cultural elites of the 1950s, became the roadmap for the youth and social movements of the 1960s.

Nowhere was this disillusionment starker then in Allen Ginsberg's poem "Howl," arguably one of the most influential American poems of the twentieth century.[12] Ginsberg begins, "I saw the best minds of my generation destroyed by madness, Starving hysterical naked, dragging themselves through the negro streets at dawn looking for an angry fix." He goes on to relate his own incredible journey through the academy and streets of New York, ravaged and debased

---

11. See especially Ken Jordan, *Evergreen Review Reader, 1957–1996* (New York: Arcade Publishing, 1994); and Ann Charters, ed., *The Portable Beat Reader* (New York: Viking Penguin Group, 1992).

12. Allen Ginsberg, *Howl and Other Poems* (San Francisco: City Lights Books, 1956), 9–20.

by the cruelties of ordinary life. William Carlos Williams described it as the journey of a man who has literally gone through hell.[13] However, Ginsberg suggests that his own saga is not unique: his cry of sorrow and loss expresses the pain of all those who toil to eke out a living in a harsh society—the activists who agitate for change, the artists and visionaries who desire a better society, the poor and racially segregated outcasts who were all blindly consigned to harrowing lives by the logic of capitalism and the go-it-on-your-own individualism of the American ethos. Ginsberg's poem expresses a belief that far from offering unfettered and glorious opportunities to "the best and the brightest," America is a repressive monolith that ostracizes and eventually crushes those who challenge the status quo.

Ginsberg concludes the poem with a long psalm-like elegy to his friend Carl Solomon, a poet and artist friend from his youth who, like Ginsberg's mother, went insane and ended up at an asylum called Rockland. This claim of solidarity and empathy with those on the absolute fringes of human society—"Carl Solomon, I am with you in Rockland"—emphatically elucidates the level of discontent with the common account of social norms. Like Jesus of Nazareth facing a society that claimed the moral high ground, Ginsberg realized that truth, morality, and the future lie with those outside the dominant culture. Finally, the inarticulate howl of an outsider—a gay, drug-using, war-protesting Hare Krishna poet—expressed the frustration of the countless people whom the American dream had left behind.

The issue of immigration in the United States is a remarkable example of people being lured by the American dream and then encountering hardship because their differences prompted people to view them as strangers. Over the centuries, each new group of immigrants—from Ireland, from China, from the Mediterranean, from Eastern Europe, from Mexico—encountered fierce discrimination from the people already established in America. These immigrants left their homelands to answer the call of the American dream, but to have any chance of realizing that dream—their dream—they needed to abandon what made them special and assimilate into the dominant culture. For example, many abandoned their native language in

---

13. William Carlos Williams, "Howl for Carl Soloman," in Ginsberg, *Howl and Other Poems*, 7–8.

the face of a strong "English only" prejudice. Ironically, a culture that esteems rugged individualism cannot tolerate difference.

What is even more ironic is that the culture that has at times portrayed itself in Christian terms as the embodiment of "God's city on the hill" ignores the biblical call to welcome and offer hospitality to the stranger. If American Christians truly envisioned a Christian utopia—that is, the establishment of God's beloved community among them in the present moment—wouldn't they accept all as equal brothers and sisters no matter their language, nation, race, or customs? Logically, this view would require Christians to see immigration—especially of refugees, the poor, and the marginalized—as a good thing that this country should cultivate. On a practical level, this should lead to the development of laws and practices that promote a more radical inclusion of people into society.

Yet there are members of our so-called Christian society who have a different vision of the beloved community. They view US society as primarily monolithic—that is, white, Anglo-Saxon, Protestant, and closed. To such a society, immigrants, particularly illegal immigrants, signify a danger and even a crisis for American society: a threat to the established "way of life," perhaps, or a spreading of precious resources among the undeserving. This fear results in restrictions that, ironically, often go against the best interests of the people who uphold them: immigrants, even illegal immigrants, can provide necessary services at very low cost.

Many Americans believe one thing and live something else. Thus, American life can be characterized as being in a constant state of contradiction. What might help heal this incoherence at the heart of society? One possibility is that a renewed aesthetics—a sense of what is beautiful and pleasing—could reorganize and clarify morality and logic and thereby help recover a plan of life that reflects actual human experience.

THE POPULARITY OF IMPRESSIONISM

French impressionism began as a revolt against the classical art tradition of the late baroque period, a tradition that emphasized precision, the classical subject matter of Greek mythology and abstract ideals, and highly complex processes of design and execution. The impressionists instead preferred to paint outdoors with bright and imaginative palettes that re-created the common objects and routines of daily life rather than refined abstract forms. They also took account of how the human eye works and how the memory and personal experience of the viewer enhances and reinterprets the work of the artist. Impressionists offered a refreshingly positive vision of the beauty in ordinary life and the natural world, but they had to struggle for acceptance and were often barred from participation in the most important and influential salons and galleries of the day.

Many Americans appreciate impressionist art; one comes across it in homes, offices, and public spaces. Impressionism may be the most beloved form of art in middle- and upper-middle-class white America. However, what is the reason for its widespread popularity?

Stripped from its original context, impressionism no longer signals a revolution in aesthetic consciousness. On the contrary, it may show something rather disconcerting about what Americans consider to be beautiful. Impressionism in America may reinforce the narcissism and moral complacency of the culture by reflecting back what Americans consider the normal life. Impressionist paintings depict white people who seem to be happy and peaceful, and celebrate daily life as important and vibrant. There is little in the way of pathos in this genre. There are no poor people, no wars, no class animosity or political acrimony. Might the beauty of Monet's water lilies reinforce American commoditization of nature, and might Renoir's children at play represent the ideal of a carefree life unaware of the suffering and despair present elsewhere?

Far from its original intention of putting people back in touch with "real" life, impressionism now may function for many as a mode of escapism in a culture walled in on all sides and shielded from the facts of history and the harsh realities that US lifestyles impose on the lives of others. It particularly removes the viewer from the prospect of death that haunts most of humanity. Impressionism in an American context is optimistic because it promotes a bright, positive, and attractive assessment of the world and its possibilities. However, it lacks hope precisely because it avoids those conditions of life out of which hope springs and without which optimism is vacuous. Is it possible that the popularity of impressionism has a connection with twenty-first oppression?

BEAUTY, RACE, AND CLASS

Virgil Elizondo, known for founding US Latino theology, asks people to consider what a society views as beautiful in order to determine the real ethos of the culture. What do those in the dominant culture consider beautiful? What do they see as ugly? What don't they see at all? Robert Coles, a sociologist and psychologist at Harvard University, undertook a study in the 1950s with young African American girls to determine their level of self-awareness and sense of self-worth.[14] The program was actually quite simple: in a controlled study the researchers asked these girls to play with the doll they considered to be most beautiful. All of the children had a black doll and a white doll to choose from. The African American girls overwhelmingly chose the white doll as the most beautiful and desirable to play with it. Follow-up conversations with the children revealed their general feeling that white people were more beautiful than black people. This shocking study demonstrated the psychological depth at which aesthetic presumptions take hold in a culture.

Fifty years later Coles repeated his study, with surprisingly similar results. This suggests that simply changing laws does not ensure real equality and that the seeds of racism are planted deeply in the subconscious American mind.

Racism persists because it has become so firmly rooted in the aesthetic sensibilities of the population. When the majority of a society views nonwhites as less than beautiful—even ugly—there will be immense social consequences. Particularly pernicious is how nonwhites accept this aesthetic vision. Perhaps even more perilous is the tendency in American life to not see nonwhites at all. Racism often makes racial minorities invisible to both the wider society and to themselves. The failure to notice another's presence is the most dehumanizing form of personal and social rejection. This was Ralph Ellison's point in writing *Invisible Man*. Invisibility represents the ultimate form of discrimination.

While American society in general views the economically poor as ugly because they are considered morally inferior and economically irrelevant, they also view the poor as invisible. That the poor are not

---

14. Robert Coles, *Children in Crisis*, vol. 1, *The Moral Life of Children* (Boston: Houghton, Mifflin Co., 1986).

present in one of the most common forms of visual art in the United States only serves to highlight the invisibility of the poor in US society as a whole. The poor have been pushed far off to the margins both psychologically and literally so that they do not tarnish the "beauty" of an illusory American dream to which many people, including the poor themselves, still cling. Because so many among the poorer members of society are nonwhite, the dominant culture tends to equate racial minority with poverty, to the extent that even upper-class nonwhites are automatically assumed to be poor and, therefore, unwelcome and dangerous. Numerous stories attest to the difficulty African American men have in hailing a taxi in a US city, for example. Because the aesthetic sensibilities underlying American culture are so exclusive, the society will not be able to move forward on race and class until it exchanges the aesthetics of optimism for the aesthetics of hope.

CONCLUSION

Americans appear to be enmeshed in a false value system that causes them to fundamentally misinterpret their lives. This false value system conforms to what the Christian tradition has generally understood to be original sin. Original sin denotes a pervasive and incipient chaos that pervades and shapes the context of all forms of perception and judgment in every human culture. Original sin is normally rooted in false interpretation of the transcendental qualities of the true, good, and beautiful. Original sin as understood in this way does not presume that the world is fundamentally depraved or evil, but that basically good intentions and goals can be subverted or inverted over time by limited and distorted tendencies and impulses. The good one intends ultimately goes awry to the point that one is caught up in lifestyles and habits of behavior and interpretations of reality that are skewed, chaotic, and self-defeating.[15]

The first part of this book analyzed a specifically American form of original sin: the nexus of false values and confused habits that wall in Americans from a truer version of reality are based on radical individualism, envy, and the lack of hope in the dominant ethos of US culture. All of this comes down to how one envisions the good life. Is

---

15. See further Murphy-O'Connor, *Becoming Human Together*, 85–105.

the good life to be identified fundamentally as happiness, momentary pleasure, and sensory enjoyment or as a life defined by moral virtue, logical clarity, and a true and vibrant vision of the future that enlivens present activity toward the good, the beautiful, and the true? If one holds the good life to be the former, one will realize quickly that one cannot easily change one's opinions. Rather, one needs to go through a deeper process of transformation and reorientation of the way that one looks at and acts in the world. This radical reorientation is essential for the attainment of the good life and is the only way of first seeing beyond and finally dismantling the walls of pharaoh's house.

The belief underlying this understanding of the morally good life has a profound impact on the way one conceives freedom. In a country that so prizes the notion of freedom, the myopic concentration on the self, the logic of the marketplace, and the lack of genuine hope paralyze and diminish the authentic freedom that individuals so desire. Freedom requires that one live not just "free from" restrictions, personal invasions, and deprivations of liberty but also "free for" love, service, and virtue. The values that many Americans embrace so uncritically often actually erode the freedom they seek most fervently. The nexus of false values create a situation in which people are imprisoned in the walls of an extremely narrow and limited world of their own creation. The goal of a process of conversion is to free people so they can pursue and experience a truly good life. Conversion enables people to see a broader realm of existence that encompasses those outside of their own cultural enclave in a way that is transformative for both themselves and their cultural enclave. This great broadening of one's horizons of existence creates a freedom and happiness that is not otherwise available to those who cannot see, hear, and feel the possibilities already present but unknown.

QUESTIONS FOR REFLECTION

1. What is the "problem of evil"? To what extent does the presence of evil in the world affect the credibility of religions that affirm belief in a loving, all-powerful God?

2. Identify concrete examples that illustrate the difference between being optimistic and hopeful, as described in this chapter. Does

the distinction between optimism and hope make sense to you? Have you personally experienced these attitudes differently?

3. How does your vision of the future affect the decisions and commitments you make?

4. Do you find US culture to be fundamentally hopeful? Why or why not? Where, if anywhere, in US cultural life do you find a lack of hopeful visions of the future?

5. How is beauty represented in the US cultural milieu? Do your experiences of beauty encourage and sustain you in any way?

6. If you are an adherent of a religion, consider whether your religion evokes hope for you. Are you familiar with religious traditions that offer powerful visions of the future, visions powerful enough to cause a person to alter the course of their life? Explain.

FOR FURTHER READING

Ali, Farhana, and Jerrold Post, "The History and Evolution of Martyrdom in Defensive Jihad: An Analysis of Suicide Bombers in Current Conflicts," *Social Research* 75, no. 2 (Summer 2008): 615–54.

Kepel, Gilles, and Peter Clark, "The Origins and Development of the Jihadist Movement: From Anti-Communism to Terrorism," *Asian Affairs* 34, no. 2 (July 2003): 91–109.

McDannell, Colleen, and Bernhard Lang, *Heaven: A History* (New Haven: Yale University Press, 1988).

Polkinghorne, J. C., *Belief in God in an Age of Science* (New Haven: Yale University Press, 1998).

———. *The End of the World and the Ends of God*, ed. J. C. Polkinghorne and M. Welker (London: Trinity International Press, 2000).

———. *The God of Hope and the End of the World* (New Haven: Yale University Press, 2002).

Rid, Thomas, and Marc Hecker, "The Terror Fringe," *Policy Review* 158 (December 2009/January 2010): 3–19.

Washington, James M., ed., *A Testament of Hope: The Essential Writings and Speeches of Martin Luther King Jr.* (San Francisco: Harper Collins, 1986).

Liberation as Conversion

Ring the bells that still can ring
Forget your perfect offering
There is a crack, a crack in everything
That's how the light gets in
— Leonard Cohen, "Anthem"

ON THE ROAD: CONVERSION AS JOURNEY

The story of Moses' conversion presents his transformation as a literal journey that takes him from the security and privilege of living in the royal household in Egypt to a pastoral life in the far-off land of Midian, then back to Egypt with the mission of rescuing his people and bringing them into a new land "flowing of milk and honey." From his initial insight of his kinship with the people of Israel to the dramatic moment of God's self-revelation in the burning bush on the mountain of Horeb, Moses moves from a vague and almost unconscious awareness that there is something wrong with "the way things are" to an urge to find his identity. This physical and psychological journey leads him to a clear and unmistakable encounter with the creator at the heart of all reality. In this encounter with God, Moses receives the mission that will define the rest of his life: to rescue his people and bring them into a new land. During his journey from Egypt to Horeb, Moses finds himself increasingly, though somewhat reluctantly, embracing a new understanding of his life and destiny that he never could have predicted or planned for as young man in the house of pharaoh. At Horeb, Moses discovers himself in a relationship with a God who expects much more of him than he ever expected of himself.

The God that Moses encounters invites him to fundamentally reinterpret his life and destiny. Moses' willingness to accept God's invitation to trust God and to follow the mission that he is given in spite of his own fear and apprehension represents what the Hebrew tradition calls faith. This is the same faith that characterizes all of the major figures in the story of the Hebrew people. This faith then is neither a single act nor a belief in an abstract idea nor a passive trust in an all-powerful God; it is a journey, a relationship with a living God grounded in trust that requires people to open their lives to a new and unknown future. This type of radical trust requires change: it requires that a person open his or her life to a process of transformation of perception, imagination, desires, expectations, loyalties, beliefs, and hopes. This faith is a journey that ultimately reshapes and reconfigures a person's life in service to God's plans. In turn, this transformation, far from robbing individuals of their autonomy, actually reveals to them their deepest gifts, talents, and possibilities.

CONVERSION IN THE CHRISTIAN TRADITION

The Christian tradition maintains that through belief in Jesus of Nazareth humans encounter God as a human person. The willingness of people to place their trust in Jesus Christ and enter into a relationship of trust—a journey—with him defines their lives. Christians call this journey discipleship. Jesus is regarded as the plan of God (he calls it the reign of God) made flesh. Saint Paul says that when people accept Jesus' invitation to follow him, they open themselves to be transformed into his image and likeness (Rom 8:14–17; 1 Cor 2:10–16; 2 Cor 3:18). This process of transformation opens people to live out more fully God's plan in a unique way in their own lives. This process also integrates every believer into the living body of Christ called the church. The pattern this process takes will differ in each human life depending on a variety of factors, such as unique personalities and gifts and social and historical conditions. However, in general, believers claim that all disciples of Jesus go through a process of personal conversion in the course of their encounter with Jesus Christ and join him on a journey through his paschal mystery—passion, death, and Resurrection. They believe that they receive his own Spirit as a source of empowerment and guide as they try to live in imitation of Jesus' life. This common journey, believers claim, unites all in the same destiny: union with the glorified Christ in the divine life of God.

The Gospels are replete with stories of conversion. Again and again ordinary people are called to break out of their set way of looking at the world and open their eyes and ears to see it and hear it the way that Jesus does. Whether through complacency, fear, or diversion, many cannot seem to break free from the status quo of their lives to follow Jesus on his mission. However, some people do accept Jesus' call and literally drop what they are doing to follow him. Often these disciples are not at first fully aware of what Jesus is asking them to do. The Gospels portray their journey of faith as a struggle to comprehend Jesus' message and to trust him completely even when they lack a full understanding of where he is leading. There are moments of genuine clarity for many of his followers when they truly "see" who Jesus is and what he represents. Peter at Caesarea Philippi realizes that Jesus is truly "the Messiah, the Son of the living God" (Mt 16:13–17). Those present at Jesus' baptism, his transfiguration, and many of his most dramatic miracles perceive God's presence in Jesus and their own lives with profound clarity. Jesus observes on a number of occasions that the poor and outcast seem especially open to seeing the reign of God and accepting its invitation. Perhaps those with the least invested in the status quo are the most open to envisioning—even hoping—that the reality of God could differ radically from what most people presume it to be. The process of conversion is at work from the initial stages of the disciples hearing Jesus' invitation, through the dramatic moments when they see and understand clearly the source and reason of their trust in Jesus, until they so internalize the mission of Jesus as their own that they effectively become "another Christ."

Although, as stated earlier, there are many patterns of conversion evident in the New Testament, there are two fairly famous examples that should be highlighted here: the one on the road to Damascus and the one on the road to Emmaus. These are not exhaustive of all of the complex ways that disciples give their lives over to Christ, but they demonstrate two primary approaches to Christian conversion.

The Road to Damascus (Acts 9:1-19)

In Luke's telling of Paul's journey, he first appears armed with warrants and "breathing threats and murder against the disciples of the Lord" (Acts 9:1). While on the road to Damascus to carry out his intentions, Paul (named Saul at this point) is struck down by a flash of light and hears a voice asking him, "Saul, Saul, why do you persecute me?" (9:4). Saul asks who is addressing him and is told, "I am Jesus, whom you are persecuting" (9:5). The voice then instructs him to get up, go into the city, and await instructions. Saul was left blinded by the experience, so his companions led him to the city to await Jesus' instructions. After three days, Jesus sends a disciple named Ananias to lay hands on Saul so that he can receive the Holy Spirit and be baptized. Ananias's presence and message from Jesus causes Saul to regain his sight and immediately desire to preach about Jesus in the local synagogues.

Paul's direct encounter with the risen Christ and almost immediate transformation into full discipleship marks a unique type of conversion experience in the New Testament. It is important to remember however, that he was already a religiously converted and very devout Jew and so he must have had a profound sense of faith in God. Evidently this faith was seriously misdirected in that it led him to hatred and violence. His shocking encounter with the risen Christ not only altered his understanding of his religious identity and mission but also helped him toward a more authentic understanding of the God he believed in. Throughout the rest of his long and complicated ministry on behalf of the reign of God, this dramatic experience would serve to reassure and guide him in the many tasks that God gave him.

Road to Emmaus (Lk 24:13-35)

This story describes two unnamed disciples of Jesus who, discouraged and confused, are leaving Jerusalem after the execution of Jesus. These pilgrims were evidently brought together by the ministry of Jesus but have been shattered by the reality of its implications. While on their way to a place called Emmaus they are joined by the risen Christ, who offers to share their journey. They do not recognize Jesus as he consoles them and helps them to interpret the events they witnessed. They invite Jesus to stay with them, even though they still do not see him for who he truly is. Finally, during their shared meal at the end of the day, they come to a full realization of the Resurrection and Christ's presence among them. Now that their "eyes" are "opened," they immediately go forth to share the news with others. In this story, the disciples' full conversion comes about only gradually, reaching its fullness when "the day is . . . nearly over."

When hearing the term *conversion*, many Christians tend to think of the dramatic revelation and transformation that characterizes Paul's story. While this experience is, in fact, replicated in the lives of many Christians through the centuries, it does not seem to be the dominant model of conversion for all Christians. Many Christians relate more directly with the unnamed disciples on the road to Emmaus, who only gradually realize the radical presence of Christ in their lives. These disciples often report that the encounter with the risen Christ "dawned" on them rather than knocking them to the ground in a blinding light. Both modes of conversion, however, are characterized by a complex process that changes the disciples' fundamental interpretation of the world and commits them to a mission that will have implications for every aspect of their lives. The process of conversion leads all those who experience it on a journey of faith that transforms them to the core of their identity. This journey allows them to move beyond the walls of ignorance and fear that entrap them, often unwittingly, in a narrow world of selfishness and sin. This process of transformation and dismantling of walls will be explored more explicitly in the following sections.

A THEOLOGY OF CONVERSION

The theology of conversion articulated here follows the pioneering work of Donald Gelpi SJ (1934–2011). Gelpi was a Jesuit priest and a professor of historical and systematic theology at the Jesuit School of Theology and the Graduate Theological Union in Berkeley, California, from 1973 through 2008.[1] Gelpi's theology is consistent with a traditional Christian interpretation of humans and their relationships to God and to others. He has also analyzed and correlated that

---

1. For autobiographical details of Gelpi's life, see Donald Gelpi, *Closer Walk: Confessions of a U.S. Jesuit* (Lanham, MD: Hamilton Books, 2006).

tradition with contemporary developments in psychology, sociology, and philosophy. His is a thoughtful examination of the process of conversion and its practical consequences for human development.

In the works of the extremely diverse body of North American thinkers,[2] Gelpi found many common threads that, woven together over time, created a uniquely American way of interpreting reality. Among the most important concepts that link these thinkers is their understanding of and reliance on experience. Americans have a long tradition of privileging individual experience and using it as the basis of rationalism and religiosity. In America, experience often provides the criteria for distinguishing between what is authentic and genuine and what is superficial or false.

Gelpi also uncovered in the works of American philosophy a profound interest in the human ability to undergo deep and sustained transformation, reorientation, and growth in most dimensions of their lives. Beginning with the pioneering work of Jonathan Edwards,[3] many American philosophers have expressed interest in the concept of conversion. Broadly speaking, *conversion* refers to the ability of an individual to adapt to changing circumstances, to develop new habits and skills, and to dramatically change her or his personality because of deeply felt emotional and intuitive experiences.

In the late 1960s, early in his career, Gelpi became involved with what became known as the Catholic Charismatic Renewal Movement. Through his involvement, Gelpi encountered an emotional and spiritual transformation characterized by a profound form of prayer and an intensely deep relationship with God. He later described this as a personal Pentecost.[4] Gelpi's personal history convinced him of

---

2. Although Gelpi developed much of his theological material in dialogue with the tradition of US pragmatism, the primary theological source for his work was a Canadian, Bernard Lonergan.

3. Jonathan Edwards (1703–1758), Puritan minister and theologian, was one of the first great intellectuals in North America. He was deeply involved in the first Great Awakening at his church in Massachusetts from 1733 to1735. For more information, see John E. Smith, *Jonathan Edwards: Puritan, Preacher, Philosopher* (Notre Dame, IN: University of Notre Dame Press, 1992).

4. Gelpi, *Closer Walk*, 165–205. For an analysis of the Catholic Charismatic Renewal Movement, see Gelpi, *Pentecostalism: A Theological Viewpoint* (Mahwah, NJ: Paulist Press, 1971) and *Pentecostal Piety* (Mahwah, NJ: Paulist Press, 1972); see also Francis A Sullivan, *Charisms and Charismatic Renewal: A Biblical and Theological Study* (Eugene, OR: Wipf and Stock, 2004).

the centrality of conversion in any theological reflection, and he came to understand that in America, conversion has a special relationship with individual experience. In this, Gelpi built upon the work of Canadian Catholic theologian and philosopher Bernard Lonergan SJ (1904–1984), who revolutionized the understanding of conversion by showing that it comes in a variety of forms and need not only occur in a religious context.[5]

Over the last twenty-five years, Gelpi grounded a theology of conversion in the intersection of the Christian tradition and the contemporary American cultural ethos.[6] In Gelpi's theology, the idea of conversion encompasses both the uniquely American form of interpreting reality and the universal process at the heart of Christianity.

CONVERSION AS BOTH INITIAL AND ONGOING

In Gelpi's synthesis, there are two main aspects of conversion: initial and ongoing.[7] According to Gelpi, the movement from irresponsibility to responsibility in some dimension of human activity is a personal conversion. The decision to take adult control of one's behavior and actions is a deliberate, conscious one.[8] There are a variety of different realms of experience over which one can determine to take control. Gelpi identifies these major areas as affective, intellectual, moral, sociopolitical, and religious. Furthermore, any change in one

---

5. Gelpi, *Closer Walk*, 162; Bernard Lonergan, *Method in Theology* (New York: Hereder and Herder, 1972). For more on the work of Bernard Lonergan, see Frederick E. Crowe, *Lonergan* (Collegeville, MN: Liturgical Press, 1992).

6. Gelpi here is endorsing the work of Bernard Lonergan in *Method*, particularly pages 57–100 and 267–93.

7. In what follows I offer my own synthesis of Gelpi's model of conversion drawing principally from three sources in which Gelpi explicitly discusses his model of conversion, although the notion of conversion and its implications underlies all of Gelpi's work: Donald L. Gelpi, *Inculturating North American Theology: An Experiment in Foundational Method* (Atlanta, GA: Scholars Press, 1988), 31–48; *Committed Worship: A Sacramental Theology for Converting Christians*, vol. 1, *Adult Conversion and Initiation* (Collegeville, MN: Liturgical Press, 1993), 1430; *The Gracing of Human Experience: Rethinking the Relationship between Nature and Grace* (Collegeville, MN: Liturgical Press, 2001), 325–36.

8. Gelpi, *Committed Worship*, 19–22.

area may lead to changes in other areas, which in turn may cause still more changes in the first area. One decision will affect future decisions in an ongoing process.

However, what causes a conversion? What factors might lead a person to need to take control of some aspect of his or her life? Generally, some event or series of events that challenges one's accepted way of life prompts a reevaluation of one's habits and interpretations. Such a disruption in one's usual judgment process can lead a person to take responsibility for bridging the disruption in some way. For instance, the pain and dysfunction caused by unresolved childhood issues may eventually lead someone to seek professional help. In seeking professional advice, that person begins taking responsibility for the affective dimension of her or his life. Likewise, persons with a narcissistic personality may at some point in life realize that exclusively self-centered activity is actually self-defeating. This realization can lead such people to question their conventional wisdom and decide that they need to take responsibility for their moral life. Once they do, they begin a process of moral conversion.

Conversions often follow a pattern popularly referred to as breakdown/breakthrough.[9] A breakdown occurs when the habitual way of interpreting events or behaving can no longer adequately account for certain experiences or feelings. When someone in breakdown decides to take responsibility for resolving the issue, a breakthrough occurs. A breakthrough opens a new way of looking at the universe; it gives one "new eyes and new ears."[10] Almost every human experiences breakdown/breakthrough at some point in life, which is to say that almost every human undergoes a conversion of some sort.

Some people, however, experience the breakdown but refuse to accept the breakthrough, choosing instead to go on living in a self-defeating way. One can choose to remain emotionally dysfunctional. One can choose to live an intellectually narrow or morally irresponsible life. Some people live a long time in an unconverted and limited way despite overwhelming evidence that their approach

---

9. For a popular description of this issue, see Matthew Fox, *Breathrough: Meister Eckhart's Creation Spirituality in New Translation* (Garden City, NY: Image Books, 1980), 302–12.

10. Gelpi, *Committed Worship*, 22.

to life is simply not working. Humans tend toward inertia and inaction in their lives rather than growth, development, and maturity. Psychologists summarize this tendency with the saying, "The sickness I know is better than the wellness I don't." Saint Paul referred to this inability to accept the breakthrough as a type of captivity or imprisonment (Rom 7:14–25). This is why Gelpi identifies conversion as an adult act.

The breakthrough just mentioned is part of the initial step of conversion. Specifically, this initial step includes the following:

- a fundamental reorientation from irresponsibility to responsibility—a willingness to be held accountable to self and others
- seeing/hearing/perceiving differently
- the breakthrough (often preceded by a breakdown of some sort)
- a movement away from habitual ways of thinking and acting

These changes are necessary, but they are only the first part of the process. For conversion to take effect, there must be an ongoing process, encompassing the following changes:

- the integration of the new orientation into the whole person
- the reshaping and reforming of other aspects of the personality
- the development of new habits, virtues, and values
- eventually, a conflict with the culture's dominant/conventional ethos

FIVE DIMENSIONS OF PERSONAL CONVERSION

Successful conversion always incorporates both initial and ongoing aspects in an integrated process of personal transformation. Gelpi divides the five forms of personal conversion into "natural" and "supernatural" forms. The natural forms are the affective, intellectual, moral, and sociopolitical conversions; the supernatural form, characterized by a person's response to a divine initiative (what theologians call *grace*), is the religious conversion.

1. Affective Conversion

Gelpi presumes that at the dawn of adulthood, all humans have had both positive and negative experiences.[11] When people respond to the world around them with fear, aggression, and defensiveness, they are acting out of emotions of self-hatred, guilt, and rage deeply enmeshed in their subconscious because of earlier negative experiences. Likewise, when people respond in friendly, empathetic, loving, and intentionally vulnerable ways, they are acting out of feelings of trust, self-worth, sympathy, and joy stemming from earlier positive experiences. Gelpi asserts that repressed negative feelings lie at the heart of most human personalities and that these emotions must be revealed and healed before the rest of a personality can be free to act spontaneously and positively. Affective conversion happens when a person takes personal responsibility for his or her emotional healing and development. By definition, then, affective conversion involves the desire and subsequent commitment to recognize, examine, and heal one's negative emotions and to reinterpret one's life in terms of the positive and hopeful.[12]

Affective conversion is a hard process, perhaps the hardest of all conversion processes, because it concerns emotions that a person may have repressed so deeply as to be unaware of them. The more repressed and unconscious these emotions are, the more power they have to dominate and enslave the rest of the personality. Repressed negative emotions can eventually suppress all positive emotions, expressing themselves in a myriad of self-destructive, dangerous, and delusional ways and totally engulf the subconscious. This is an erosion of authentic personal freedom that is often called mental illness.[13]

There exist many physiological and largely somatic causes of emotional illnesses. For instance, clinical depression, bipolar disorder, and schizophrenia often result from chemical imbalances or neurological disorders largely independent of any direct psychological trauma. In other words, an individual can suffer from acute mental

---

11. Gelpi, *The Gracing of Human Experience*, 322–23.

12. Gelpi, *Committed Worship*, 17.

13. Gelpi, *Gracing of Human Experience*, 282–96. Gelpi, *Inculturating North American Theology*, 134–38.

disorders because of medical conditions not caused by that person's psychological development. Diseases of this type can be treated with medications and therapies and are not dependent on psychological examination and reintegration. Nevertheless, even physiologically rooted disorders require the affected persons to decide to take control of the somatic-psychological dimensions of their lives, to accept healing medication, and to reinterpret life in terms of an altered ability to evaluate reality.

The great American writer Flannery O'Connor once said that anybody who survives childhood has enough information about life to last a lifetime.[14] The first twenty-some years of any human life is a jumble of confused and conflicting emotions that can take a lifetime to unpack, clarify, and understand. No one enters adulthood without some level of psychological chaos and repression. Left unresolved, these subconscious negative emotions can fester and mutate until they skewer one's view of reality, create unhealthy habits and personality traits, and subvert any good and positive tendencies one might possess. Some degree of emotional breakdown of the type mentioned earlier is relatively common in human experience. If a person does not take advantage of the breakdown to achieve a breakthrough, the negative emotions will eventually overwhelm the conscious attitudes.

In Gelpi's view, aesthetic (what one sees as beautiful or pleasing) appreciation can serve as an important catalyst for change and growth in the affective dimension of any human life. Sensing the presence of beauty in one's life can actually be a life-changing breakthrough, an awakening of desire for a more positive, richer, and deeper emotional life. Helping to place one's experience in a broader context, an aesthetic appreciation can become a way of integrating the past into a hopeful vision of the future.

A person interested in reflecting on one's life in relation to Gelpi's understanding of affective conversion can use the following questions:

- Have I genuinely taken responsibility for my own personal emotional and psychological well-being?

---

14. Flannery O'Connor, "The Nature and Aim of Fiction," in *Mystery and Manners*, ed. Sally and Robert Fitzgerald (New York: Ferrar, Straus, and Giroux, 1961), 84.

- Have I honestly and constructively confronted my personal pain, dysfunctions, limitations, and conscious and unconscious fears and anxieties?
- Do I like myself? Do I think of myself as a good and valuable person?
- Have I confronted and dealt with my painful memories from childhood? How do these affect my interpersonal relationships now?
- What dysfunctions existed in my family of origin? Do I manifest these same dysfunctions? If so, how do I control these?
- Am I generally happy and optimistic? Is my happiness real or a cover?
- Does anyone know the real me? Would I want anyone to?
- Do I feel no need to control factors external to me: other people, my environment, situations that are not my direct responsibility?
- Do I feel no need to "save" and "fix" other people?
- Do I have some appreciation of art, music, literature, or some other form of beauty? Have I developed my own artistic and creative possibilities and talents?
- Do I generally experience the amount and level of affection and intimacy that I feel I need?

2. Intellectual Conversion

Intellectual conversion involves taking responsibility for the truth or falsity of one's beliefs by examining and testing them in the light of perspectives and frames of reference differing from one's own.[15] In so doing, a person opens to ongoing clarification, revision, and transformation.

An initial intellectual conversion often simply involves the realization that other frames of reference exist, have validity, and make necessary claims on one's attention. Ongoing intellectual conversion, on the other hand, delivers individuals into a world of genuine systematic inquiry. Intellectual conversion requires one to adopt

---

15. Gelpi, *Gracing of Human Experience*, 295–96.

an attitude of "contrite fallibleness" that acknowledges the limited nature of one's personal view of the world.[16] A person comes to recognize that interpreting reality is an ongoing personal and social process that can only approximate truth but can never fully define it in terms of any single articulation.

People who are actively engaged in an ongoing process of intellectual conversion exhibit a love of truth that transcends any particular belief they might hold. The love of truth inspires curiosity, nurtures intellectual flexibility, and encourages people to explore unfamiliar ideas or areas of knowledge outside their normal fields of expertise, opening them to unexpected surprises. In response, people become willing to change not only their thinking but also their actions. Truth itself becomes the ultimate goal.[17]

Intellectual conversion can be identified using the following questions:

- Have I taken responsibility for my own rational judgments? Have I moved beyond conventional wisdom, or do I take most things for granted?
- Do I tend to or want to see things in "black and white"? How am I at dealing with the "gray"?
- Do I tend to challenge the group presuppositions? Do I tend to see alternatives other than those most commonly offered and generally accepted?
- Do I deal well with diversity of opinion, even when it is in an area of great concern to me?
- Do I consider other points of view before making a judgment? Do I generally know what the other points of view are? Do I want to know what they are?
- What are my areas of special competence and expertise? Do I desire to continue learning and growing in these areas, or do I feel like I know about enough?
- How many fundamental shifts in thinking have I undergone in life? In the last year?

---

16. Ibid., 143–44.

17. Gelpi, *Committed Worship*, 17, 25.

3. Moral Conversion

Moral conversion entails taking personal responsibility for one's actions and their consequences. Accountability is the key. One is accountable to oneself by choosing values that one wants to embody in all the dimensions of life and by shaping one's moral conduct according to those values. One is held accountable to others by acknowledging the social and communal dimensions of life and collaborating with others in ways that yield the good life for all. According to Gelpi, living a life directed by a vision of right action creates the foundation for genuine individuality and authentic adulthood. In other words, moral conversion serves as the key to natural freedom.[18]

What happens when a person has not experienced a moral conversion? As children often do when struggling with moral decisions and crises, a person without any clear vision of how to determine right action tries to negotiate between competing moral claims made on them by friends, family, society, religion, popular culture, and so forth. More often than not, those who have not had a moral conversion opt for the moral choice that is easiest or most expedient, without trying to determine whether this action is consistent with their other choices or with their ideals.

Before a moral conversion, people tend to follow conventional morality uncritically, by force of habit, but adult moral conversion begins when one accepts particular moral claims on one's behavior.[19] Ongoing moral conversion moves people to cultivate habits that embody the moral virtues they have embraced and to live according to a broader social responsibility. Motivated by a love of the good, a morally converted person understands that his or her good depends on the good of the community.

Gelpi positions this type of moral vision as the "golden rule": treat other people as you want to be treated. Authentic moral conversion means accepting certain external codes of conduct that presume rights for all and require duties from all. These norms of behavior evolve through social dialogue, help to ensure that the individual does not benefit at the expense of the community, and

---

18. Gelpi, *Committed Worship*, 17–23.

19. Gelpi, *Gracing of Human Experience*, 256–60.

likewise guard that the community does not enrich itself by subjugating the individual.[20]

Because human lives are profoundly interconnected, the moral conversion of one person strongly affects the moral lives of others in the community. Human behavior is imitative, and a fully morally converted person becomes a model, showing others how to take responsibility for their own lives in a similar way. It goes without saying that the lack of moral conversion by the members of a community similarly impacts the social life of all.[21]

Moral conversion can be identified using the following questions:

- Have I moved beyond a stage of conventional morality? Have I taken personal responsibility for my life and actions, or do I depend on others to tell me what to do or what is right and wrong?
- In my day-to-day activities, do I consistently follow a set of principles and values that I have freely chosen?
- Do I act the same when I am in public as when I am alone and "no one will ever know"?
- Do I have a strong desire for personal integrity? Do I admire it in others?
- Do I cultivate virtues and develop habits that enable me to live by the principles and values that I hold?
- Do I acknowledge and confront my inconsistent behavior, or do I tend to rationalize it?

4. Sociopolitical Conversion

In the course of his investigations, Gelpi became aware of the fundamental difference between personal moral responsibility and the responsibility for dynamics that affect the good of those beyond one's immediate social circle.[22] The willingness to confront unjust social structures, change political discourse, and improve the general

---

20. Ibid.
21. Ibid.
22. Gelpi, *Committed Worship*, 45–55.

conditions so as to ensure the flourishing of human dignity requires a much greater commitment than the personal moral decision to treat others as you want to be treated. Sociopolitical conversion is a movement out of the personal and into the political sphere. By making such a move, a person indicates that she or he accepts responsibility to seek the good for all humans and to work strategically with others to challenge and convert the wider world as well. The Christian tradition describes this vision of universal human dignity as the common good.[23]

Many morally good people fail to undergo sociopolitical conversion. Even those engaged in extreme acts of economic domination, social upheaval, and political malfeasance often love their children and are good to their family and friends. More frequently, many remain morally unmoved and largely unaware of war, genocide, economic strangulation, or other violations of human rights. Ignorance of the wider world is itself a sign that one has not undergone a sociopolitical conversion. The initial conversion involves the often frightening idea that one has some personal responsibility for the wider world of sin, violence, and injustice that exists outside of one's particular experience—and the realization that one has some power (however limited initially) to improve the social order. Ongoing sociopolitical conversion leads one to develop relationships and strategies for challenging and changing those injustices in which one participates corporately, even unwittingly.

One cannot change the world alone. An individual cannot even change the world in a lifetime. Only by uniting one's personal efforts with those of many, many others over long historical periods can one hope to affect genuine and lasting social change. Such sustained efforts require that all members of the communal process share a hope and a vision of the common good that transcends any merely personal forms of conduct.

Sociopolitical conversion can be identified using the following questions:

- Have I moved beyond the conventional stage of sociopolitical consciousness? Do I see myself as significantly connected with

---

23. For a good explanation of the common good, see Daniel Groody, *Globalization, Spirituality and Justice* (Maryknoll, NY: Orbis Books, 2007), especially 106–9.

people different and distant from my own socioeconomic class and myself?

- Do I have a real sense of compassion? Do I have an urgent, pressing sense of justice?
- Am I generally interested in the problems of people who "don't concern me"?
- Do I ever question the status quo, or do I just assume "that's the way things are"?
- Is there any issue larger than my own personal self-interest for which I would risk ridicule, imprisonment, or my life?
- How much personal responsibility do I take for other people's suffering? Am I paralyzed by this, or do I see it as a mandate or challenge for action?
- If I have a personal prayer life, how much of it revolves around issues of justice and discernment of political action?

5. Religious Conversion[24]

Religious conversion involves the dimension of the personality that infuses meaning through other dimensions of one's life. In the initial process of religious conversion, one comes to understand that some purpose to life demands one's attention. This insight obliges one to reconsider one's whole interpretation of life and to reorder one's habitual responses accordingly. The religiously converted become aware of a sense of hope, begin to trust in the world's ultimate goodness, and develop an all-pervading sense that they are not alone. People who have religious conversions tend to affirm that there exists some broader, all-inclusive existence that wants to have a personal relationship with every human person. This existence desires and invites believers to reorient their life toward the presence of this higher power, or God. An authentic religious conversion, however, does not *initially* lead to an assent of particular religious beliefs or doctrines; in fact, a religious experience often challenges the foundational beliefs and confessional practices in which one was raised. Initial religious conversion can be characterized not so much as humans

---

24. Gelpi most fully and systematically explains his model of religious and Christian conversion in *The Gracing of Human Experience*, 315–59.

believing in God as believing that God believes in them. As Søren Kierkegaard aptly expressed, faith is a relationship that enables us to live with uncertainty without despairing.[25]

The ongoing process of religious conversion involves a systematic reinterpretation of all the dimensions of one's life—affective, intellectual, moral, and sociopolitical—in terms of this radical new relationship that one has chosen to accept. A review of the past gives one a new vision of the future, one that provides a deepened sense of purpose and direction in the present. The religious convert's "new eyes and new ears" reveal the full scope of life's possibilities. Most of all, religious conversion gives converts an abiding sense that some divine presence cares about their choices, guides their deliberations, and promises to be with them and even deliver them in some way from the most frightening aspects of human life.

In a Christian framework, religious conversion means that a person senses the intervening presence of God (grace) calling him or her into a profoundly personal relationship with the God revealed by Jesus Christ, a triune God that a human can only imperfectly understand as a divine community of persons that both created and will ultimately reconcile all things. As usually explained, the third person in this trinity (the Holy Spirit) makes believers aware and desirous of conforming to the image of the second person (Jesus Christ). To be conformed into Christ's image necessarily puts believers in a direct and providential relationship with the first person (revealed by Jesus as "Abba," an affectionate term for father in Jesus' native language).

Ongoing Christian conversion enables individuals to fully integrate God's plan for the whole of creation, as revealed by Jesus Christ through his life and the mystery of his death and Resurrection (the paschal mystery), into his or her own personal life. The more that people are converted to Christ, the more they become like Christ in their loving and radically inclusive embrace of all people. Converted Christians urgently desire that all people experience their full human dignity (justice). Furthermore, they want to enter into life-giving relationships not only with the people they already love but even with the people they don't know or find frightening. To love as Christ loves means, ultimately, to love even one's enemies and

---

25. See Soren Kierkegaard, *The Sickness Unto Death*, trans. Walter Lowrie (New York: Doubleday Anchor Books, 1954), 212-13.

to share one's own life with strangers and those in most need of the unique talents every person possesses.

Religious conversion can be identified using the following questions:

- Have I moved beyond a stage of conventional or cultural religiosity?
- Have I had any direct or powerful experience of grace or the divine that has significantly changed or reordered my life?
- Do I have a deep sense of God's providence even if I can't understand what it is?
- Do I feel like I can trust the world and creation in general, or are they dangerous and untrustworthy?
- Do I believe that there are other valid experiences and interpretations of God and reality beside my own?
- Does my faith enable and empower me to live in a significantly new way?
- How does my faith affect other dimensions of my life?
- If I have truly had a religious conversion, how has this changed me?
- What ethical and discipleship demands have I appropriated?
- How has my prayer life been affected?
- If I have had a specifically Christian conversion, do I have a personal relationship with every member of the Trinity and the Trinity as a whole?
- Can I distinguish between what is essential and what is not in my religious expression of faith?
- Have I fully integrated myself into and committed myself to a community of shared faith? How has this changed my life?

THE DYNAMICS OF PERSONAL CONVERSION

Each type of conversion fosters and reinforces other forms of conversion. Simultaneously, the absence of conversion at some level tends to distort and even subvert the presence of conversion at another level.[26]

---

26. There are numerous places in which Gelpi discusses the dynamics and counter-dymanics of conversion, but for his most concise account, see *The Gracing of Human Experience*, 294–314.

Affective conversion *animates* the other forms of conversion, enabling one to respond flexibly, creatively, hopefully, and enthusiastically to the duties and demands that other forms of conversion entail. A healthy psychological perspective gives one the stability to face life's difficulties and to embrace these challenges as possibilities. Emotionally unhealthy people, on the other hand, dread and resist change. Because affectively unconverted persons have not accepted the task of healing their repressed pain or guilt or the distorted feelings they may have unconsciously inherited from family and society, they are not free to accept the ambiguity required for honest intellectual inquiry or the humility to entertain different and often conflicting viewpoints. Affective conversion frees a person to develop a conscience and to trust it when confronted with hard moral choices. It endows a person with a keen sense of empathy and compassion. It also gives an intuitive vision of the beautiful and excellent possibilities of this life. Using the process of psychological healing to discern the struggles and suffering of others, affective conversion suffuses sociopolitical conversion with a sense of urgency and hopefulness.

Intellectual conversion orders the other forms of conversion by training them to think clearly and correctly about any type of experience. Intellectual conversion provides ever-deepening insights about how one *ought* to feel and *ought* to act, mediating a healthy interaction between one's affect, one's intellect, and one's moral reasoning. Intellectual conversion also trains the mind to reflect on religious experience and judge whether certain expressions of religious beliefs are healthy or unhealthy. The lack of intellectual conversion leaves people in disordered confusion, prone to authoritarianism, fundamentalism, dogmatism, and nihilism.

Both moral and sociopolitical conversions help orient the other forms of conversion toward beliefs and values that make absolute claims. Because all forms of conversion entail taking responsibility for some realm of personal experience, each one changes the way a person acts and reacts over time. A healthy affect and a well-functioning intellect create the conditions for the development of a vibrant conscience that allows a person to engage in critical examination of his or her moral claims and duties. This emerging conscience informs all other aspects of experience with a broader purpose and general categories of right and wrong. A working conscience would conclude that having the knowledge to make vast and dangerous biological weapons does not mean that one should make them. A moral vision of the good gives one the eyes to see the beauty of other people and their unique cultures and the ears to hear truthful claims and moral demands that these people are allowed to make.

Sociopolitical conversion deprivatizes the other forms of conversion by "actively consecrating one to some just cause of universal human import which involves one publicly in the struggle for a just social order."[27] All the other forms of conversion require some cause to which ones devotes one's heart and mind over the course of a lifetime. While this cause can emerge out of religious experience, it goes beyond personal belief and engenders social activism on behalf of others. In the United States, the break between others types of conversion—particularly religious conversion—and sociopolitical activism is most pronounced. Sociopolitical conversion ultimately authenticates genuine religious conversion by producing a real action that expresses the greater good of all creation desired by God. Sociopolitical conversion also brings the social dimensions of the other conversions into new fullness by bringing people into a shared community of purpose—that is, working for a goal that is greater than any individual human life or destiny.

Religious conversion transvalues affective, intellectual, moral, and sociopolitical conversion. In Gelpi's analysis, *transvaluing* means shifting the fundamental frame of reference in which one experiences affective, speculative, and moral conversion, in a way that casts all experience in a new light.[28] When there is a shift in a fundamental frame of reference, all dimensions of the personality will be reshaped in reference to this new perspective. Religious conversion transvalues affective conversion by calling it to graced repentance and giving it "radiant hope." It transvalues intellectual conversion by requiring that one develop a new critical self-understanding of one's own life and world in terms of the revelation of faith. In Christian terms, one begins to measure the world against the revelation of the Word made flesh in Jesus Christ, his own guiding and interpreting Spirit that he

---

27. Gelpi, *Gracing of Human Experience*, 297.

28. Gelpi, *Inculturating North American Theology*, 39.

pours out on all believers, and the texts and rituals of remembrance that emerged out of the community of faith that Christ and the Spirit created. When one's affect and intellect are religiously transvalued, the possibility of true wisdom—a virtue greatly prized by the ancients—tends to emerge.

Religious conversion also transvalues moral conversion by ensuring that revealed truths inform the human conscience. In Christian terms, the believer needs to conform his or her mind to the mind of Christ—to imitate the vision of the beloved community and the virtues it requires. Religious conversion transvalues sociopolitical conversion by uniting its absolute goals and principles with the revealed divine plan for all creation. Sociopolitical conversion serves as the authenticating mark of religious conversion, and religious conversion gives sociopolitical aspirations a divine mandate and the inspiring hope of God's own collaboration with and vindication of the greater good that one chooses. In Christian terms, the vision of the beloved community inspires and directs all activities resulting from sociopolitical conversion.

Gelpi takes pains to explain the fundamental difference between the four natural forms of conversion and religious conversion instigated and directed by supernatural grace. All natural forms of conversion are possible without the presence or acknowledgment of divine grace, and religious conversion can take place in isolation from the other forms of conversion. On the other hand, religious conversion alone without other forms of natural conversion can devolve into narcissism, fundamentalism, and activities that use religion as a weapon to attack others and impose a particular ideology. Similarly, natural conversions without a broader religious frame of reference can lack the wise enlightenment and authentic zeal that divine revelation and its attendant gifts of faith, hope, and love supply. In Christian understanding, the goal of all conversion ultimately needs to be integral holistic conversion, a full transformation of each person into the divine image by which and for which humans were created.

CONCLUSION

Moving beyond the walls of pharaoh's house requires an integral adult conversion. An integral adult conversion is seldom either simple or instantaneous but instead requires that one enter into a complex process of change and reorientation in multiple areas of one's personal life. Holistic conversion transforms people in every dimension of their lives. At a minimum, holistic conversion requires that people experience at least an initial level of conversion in all five of the areas of conversion that Gelpi names, and that this initial level of conversion affects and is integrated into other aspects of life and personality. Furthermore, as Gelpi insists, Christian conversion requires that people move beyond simply believing in some higher power or God that gives direction and purpose to the universe. Conversion to the God of Jesus Christ enables a person to accept Jesus' vision of God and God's plan for the world: the reign of God. Faith in the Christian God transvalues the other areas of conversion and obligates believers to imitate Jesus in their own lives. This desire to imitate Jesus propels Christians into on ongoing process or journey of conversion that gives each one a mission of service to the reign of God. The primary goal of this mission for those in North America is to dismantle the walls of pharaoh's house so that all people can find a true home within the wider human community that Jesus called the Reign of God.

QUESTIONS FOR REFLECTION

1. Have you or someone you know experienced a change that might be termed a conversion? If so, does the experience reflect the pattern of conversion from either Acts 9:1–19 (road to Damascus) or Luke 24:13–35 (road to Emmaus)? Explain.

2. Prior to reading this chapter, had you thought of conversion as applying to dimensions of human life other than the spiritual? Does this broad understanding of conversion offer a helpful way to analyze personal experience? Why or why not?

3. Identify stories, from novels, films, or other media, that demonstrate one or more of the types of conversion presented in this chapter and briefly explain how the stories demonstrate conversion.

5. According to Gelpi, what is the relationship between religious conversion and a person's participation in a religious tradition? Do you agree with Gelpi? Why or why not?

6. Describe Gelpi's explanation of the dynamic interrelationship of the dimensions of conversion. Is one type of conversion fundamental in the sense that without it the other types are not possible? Why or why not?

7. How does religious conversion transvalue other dimensions of conversion according to Gelpi? Identify an example of this phenomenon.

FOR FURTHER READING

Doran, Robert M., "The Nonviolent Cross: Lonergan and Girard on Redemption," *Theological Studies* 71 (2010): 46–61.

———. *Psychic Conversion and Theological Foundations*, Marquette Studies in Theology, No. 51 (Milwaukee, WI: Marquette University Press, 2006).

Gelpi, Donald, *Closer Walk: Confessions of a U.S. Jesuit* (Lanham, MD: Hamilton Books, 2006).

———. *Committed Worship: A Sacramental Theology for Converting Christians*, Vol. 1, *Adult Conversion and Initiation* (Collegeville, MN: Liturgical Press, 1993), 14–30.

———. *The Conversion Experience: A Reflective Process for RCIA Participants and Others* (Mahwah, NJ: Paulist Press, 1998).

———. *The Firstborn of Many: A Christology for Converting Christians*, Vol. 1 (Milwaukee: Marquette University Press, 2001).

———. *The Gracing of Human Experience: Rethinking the Relationship between Nature and Grace* (Collegeville, MN: Liturgical Press, 2001).

———. *Inculturating North American Theology: An Experiment in Foundational Method* (Atlanta, GA: Scholars Press, 1988), 31–48.

———. *Pentecostal Piety* (New York: Paulist Press, 1972).

―――. *Pentecostalism: A Theological Viewpoint* (New York: Paulist Press, 1971).

―――. *The Spirit in the World* (Wilmington, DE: Michael Glazier Press, 1988).

Rambo, Lewis R., *Understanding Religious Conversion* (New Haven: Yale University Press, 1995).

Sullivan, Francis A., *Charisms and Charismatic Renewal: A Biblical and Theological Study* (Eugene, OR: Wipf and Stock, 2004).

Religious Conversion in America

We cannot love God unless we love each other, and to love we must know each other. We know Him in the breaking of the bread, and we know each other in the breaking of the bread, and we are not alone any more. Heaven is a banquet and life is a banquet, too, even with a crust, where there is companionship.

We have all known the long loneliness and we have learned that the only solution is love and that love comes with community.

— DOROTHY DAY, *THE LONG LONELINESS*[1]

THE "PROBLEM" OF GOD IN AMERICA

At this point, the text examines the issues of religious conversion more closely; particularly as it pertains to the North American cultural milieu, especially the United States. Traditionally academic courses on theology examine the "problem of God," meaning, usually, an investigation into arguments of whether God exists and what this implies for human moral life. In the United States today, the "problem of God" seems not to be *whether* God exists, but *which* God exists. As the Baylor Religion Survey observes,

> American religion seems monolithic. In fact, under the surface American religion is startlingly complex and diverse.

---

1. Dorothy Day, *The Long Loneliness* (San Francisco: Harper and Row, 1952), 286.

Americans may agree that God exists. They do not agree about what God is like, what God wants for the world, or how God feels about politics. Most Americans pray. They differ widely on to whom they pray, what they pray about, and whether or not they say grace. A vast majority of Americans are Christians, but attitudes amongst those Christians regarding the salvation of others, the role of religion in government, the reality of the paranormal, and their consumption of the media are surprisingly diverse.[2]

If 90 percent of Americans believe in a God and almost that many pray at least weekly, and if almost 90 percent of Americans align themselves with a religion and more than half of them attend religious services at least monthly,[3] then it would appear that most Americans have undergone a religious conversion. However, Americans give widely divergent accounts of the manner and consequences of their religious conversion.[4] Why do people have such different interpretations of their interactions with God, and why do people have such diverse understandings of God, even the Christian God?

At the heart of the American problem of God lie two distinct factors: one concerns the nature of religious experience and its consequences; the other is that there are multiple and often incommensurable understandings of the nature and character of God.

THE TRUE NATURE OF RELIGIOUS EXPERIENCE: ROYCE CONTRA JAMES

At the turn of the last century, the Harvard philosopher William James published one of his most popular and influential works, *The Varieties of Religious Experience.*[5] His study synthesized an American

---

2. "American Piety in the 21st Century: New Insights into the Depth and Complexity of Religion in the US," Baylor Religion Survey, Baylor University (Waco, TX: Baylor Institute for Studies of Religion, 2006), 4–5.

3. Ibid., 8–13.

4. Ibid., 14–16, 22–25.

5. James, *The Varieties of Religious Experience* (New York: New American Library, 1958). Published from the Gifford Lectures of 1901–1902.

intellectual tradition that stretched back to the seventeenth century and the first Great Awakening as well as incorporating both Protestant and Roman Catholic accounts of prayer, mysticism, and spirituality. James's analysis was immensely successful and came to represent the predominant view of scholars and ordinary people alike. Nevertheless, many of the issues he framed remain unresolved and still have resonance in contemporary American culture.

Many readers of James admired the accessibility and clarity of his analysis in *The Varieties of Religious Experience*. His contemporary philosophers and friends Charles Sanders Peirce and Josiah Royce, however, viewed James's account as inadequate. Royce found the framework of James's analysis to be misdirected because it focused on the fruits of religious experience rather than the foundational and universal process of religious experience. In other words, Royce believed that James limited his research to the variety of ways in which people respond to a religious experience and did not explore the more complex dynamics of human interaction with the divine presence. In *The Sources of Religious Insight*,[6] Royce challenged James's account of religious experience as superficial and offered an alternative account of what he termed *religious insight*, which he believed more adequately describes the psychological subtlety of the preconscious and conscious stages of human interaction with God's gracious self-communication.

In brief, James described religious experience as a sudden sense of the presence of some life greater than self, an awakening that changes one's entire outlook and expresses itself in new ways of living. The mystical events in the lives of historic religious figures would be examples. In his analysis, James concluded that the apperception of something *more* and the willing submission to it are common across human cultures. The religious institutionalization of the experience, however, depends on the cultural milieu in which the experience takes place. The communities that subsequently gather tend to diminish the individual and pre-rational experience. The primary locus of the Spirit is in the private, individual human consciousness.

---

6. Josiah Royce, *The Sources of Religious Insight* (New York: Charles Scribner's Sons, 1912).

Royce, on the other hand, contends that the foundational religious experience is not a felt sense of presence or an intuitive relationship with some higher life but a direct feeling that humans *need* just such a relationship, that they *need* the divine to give meaning to their lives.[7] Individual religious experience is like Dorothy Day's "long loneliness": it only reveals the intense desire to find a way forward and awakens the hope that some outside being or thing can empower humans. However, it cannot reveal the "Deliverer." A true experience of and insight into the Deliverer comes only through social experience—connection to other humans—because the need for salvation is common to all. A real religious experience is an awareness that individuals are not alone because of their human relationships. For Royce, this experience is not supernatural but is entirely natural.[8] Any mystical experience is the fruit and not the source of this type of experience.[9]

Because for Royce the term *religious experience* implies a spontaneous intuition that excludes or overrides reason, he prefers the term *religious insight*, which includes both immediate experience and rational analysis:

> Insight is a name for a special sort and degree of knowledge . . . knowledge that makes us aware of the unity of many facts in one whole, and that at the same time brings us into intimate personal contact with these facts and with the whole wherein they are united. The three marks of insight are breadth of range, coherence and unity of view, and closeness of personal touch. . . .[10]
> . . . True insight, if fulfilled, would be empirical for it would face facts; intuitive, for it would survey them and grasp them, and be intimate with them; rational for it would view them in their unity.[11]

---

7. Ibid., 46–54.

8. Ibid., 52, 74.

9. There is a strong correlation with Royce's insight in the autobiographical reflection of Dorothy Day: "We have all known the long loneliness and we have learned that the only solution is love and that love comes with community." Dorothy Day, *The Long Loneliness* (San Francisco: Harper and Row, 1952), 286.

10. Royce, *Sources of Religious Insight*, 5–6.

11. Ibid., 102.

In the classic Christian model of religious conversion, Saint Augustine realized he needed an intellectual conversion to properly interpret what God is calling him to be. The conversion process cannot be sundered from a critical reflection on the implications of one's religious impulses.[12]

In Royce's view, the institutional aspects of religion are expressions of the divine because they can be a source of meaning and purpose. The highest forms of religious insight are not personal but come about through the loyal dedication of the individual to a cause embodied in a religious community. Such insight enables individuals to commit themselves to the community and its Spirit even to the point of suffering and death. At the same time, although an individual needs a community to be saved, communities themselves are also in need of salvation, which can come about only through a humble openness to the Spirit guiding them through repentance and renewal. A community that is not engaged is this complex process of transformation cannot find salvation for itself or the individuals that comprise it.

While religious insight grows through shared reflection, prayer, and discernment, the struggle against evil, sin, and suffering can be a rich source of religious insight.[13] The presence of evil confronts each person with a choice: either to acquiesce to this evil or to oppose it. In resisting evil, one encounters the divine presence working to unite one's efforts to the wider universal process of resistance and reconciliation; and in renouncing evil, one understands that grace and sin are inextricably interwoven in ways that lead to transformation, not only in spite of but often because of evil deeds. While never condoning evil, religious insight suggests that a greater good can, and often does, emerge through active resistance to sin and suffering.

In Royce's analysis, religious insight culminates in unification with the universal Beloved Community: a life-changing commitment to divine solidarity enables a person to experience the fullness of universal salvation. It initiates one into the divine community that is God. The

---

12. See further Augustine of Hippo, *The Confessions and Enchiridion*, trans. and ed. Albert Outler (Grand Rapids, MI: Christian Classics Ethereal Library, 1955), chapters 4–7.

13. Donald Gelpi, *The Gracing of Human Experience: Rethinking the Relationship between Nature and Grace* (Collegeville, MN: Liturgical Press, 2000), 186–87; Royce, *Sources of Religious Insight*, 79–116.

Christian scriptures insist that one cannot truly know and love God without knowing and loving other humans (1 Jn 4:19–21). In Christian understanding, divine solidarity places one in an ever-expanding communion of communities that ultimately become the divine communion; and when one is firmly committed to universal solidarity, one enters into the everlasting process of God's own life.

THE GOD AMERICANS BELIEVE IN

Given the process of religious insight that Royce outlined, it makes sense that there are many different and often incommensurable interpretations of God. In America, communities of faith come from a wide diversity of backgrounds, with unique histories and traditions of religious interpretation. Members of each community may be more or less dedicated to common ideals and may, therefore, also have differing insights, exhibiting both the strengths and limitations of that community, adding to its development or impeding its deeper insight.

The problem of God for Christians in America is largely a problem of diverse and often competing interpretations of what they regard as revelation. Much of the time, these interpretations misconstrue authentic Christian interpretations of God, with the result that America's dominant ethos, while exhibiting a strong and devout sense of religious piety, increasingly misrepresents the Christian tradition. The many "gods," that is, the many interpretations of God that Christians in the United States embrace, are ideologically too narrow to explain the full mystery of salvation as attested to in Christian sources. "False gods" that fail to sound the call to universal solidarity that Jesus embodied, produce a panoply of misguided expressions of religious experience. Authentic religious insight—and hence religious conversion—remains elusive and sometimes unattainable.

The Baylor Religion Survey mentioned earlier asked twenty-nine questions about the character and behavior of God. The answers illuminated two distinct dimensions of belief. The first dimension deals with beliefs about the extent of God's level of *engagement* in human history and personal lives.[14] The second dimension deals with beliefs

---

14. Baylor Religion Survey, 26.

about God's level of *anger* about human affairs and the reality of sin. The survey identified four types of believers in America.

Type A: Authoritarian God. Individuals tend to think that God is highly involved in their daily lives and world affairs. They believe that God helps them make decisions and is also responsible for global events such as economic upturns or tsunamis. They feel that God is quite angry and is capable of meting out punishment to those who are unfaithful or ungodly.

Type B: Benevolent God. Believers tend to think that God is very active in their daily lives, but they are less likely to believe that God is angry and acts in wrathful ways. For these believers, the Benevolent God is mainly a force of positive influence in the world, less inclined to condemn or punish individuals.

Type C: Critical God. Believers feel that God really does not interact with the world. Nevertheless, God still observes humans and views the current state of the world unfavorably. These individuals feel that they will know God's displeasure in another life ,and that divine justice may not be of this world.

Type D: Distant God. Believers think that God is not active in the world and not especially angry either. These individuals tend to think about God as a cosmic force that set the laws of nature in motion. God does not "do" things in the world and does not hold clear opinions about human activities or world events.[15]

Almost two-thirds of Americans believe that God is fundamentally authoritative, distant, and critical.[16] This means that the majority of Americans characterize God in fundamentally negative terms. Although half of the people surveyed view God as engaged in human affairs, the majority of all people surveyed believe that the level of God's anger is high or very high. This view suggests that in the deepest recesses of the human consciousness, most Americans are scared of God.

Although one-quarter of the respondents believe that God is engaged and benevolent, this group overwhelmingly supports capital punishment, and only 38 percent believe that good people should

---

15. Ibid. The report also noted the existence of self-described atheists, but their views do not factor into this survey. For an analysis of self-described atheists, see "Global Index of Religion and Atheism" WIN-Gallup International, 2012, *redcresearch. ie/wp-content/uploads/2012/08/RED-C-press-release-Religion-and-Atheism-25-7-12.pdf.*

16. Baylor Religion Survey, 27.

"actively seek social and economic justice."[17] Even the majority of those who espouse belief in a compassionate and personally present, loving God have not had a sociopolitical conversion and may, in fact, experience merely a personal, therapeutic form of spirituality.[18]

While the survey concludes that religious beliefs have a strong impact on the moral attitudes of Americans, these attitudes tend toward narrowly personal morality rather than a more expansive view of the sociopolitical implications of belief. Nevertheless, more than half of those surveyed believe that the government has some responsibility to distribute wealth more evenly, regulate business, and protect the environment (82 percent).[19] The most socially conscious and politically progressive believers are those who view God as distant.[20]

All of these God-types have their roots in the long Judeo-Christian tradition, as well as in the history of American thought and culture. It is possible to propose some hypotheses about the foundation of these beliefs in the American consciousness. Types A (Authoritarian God), B (Benevolent God), and C (Critical God) have clear antecedents in the fundamental neo-Calvinist understanding of God that was widespread among the Puritans and the colonial religiosity that gave birth to the United States. The many revival movements that spread throughout the country in the nineteenth and early twentieth centuries further disseminated these types. The emergence of biblical fundamentalism in the 1920s formalized and unified these many diverse strains of popular piety into a general movement in American religion.[21] Types A, B, and C also are grounded in the type of Catholic spirituality that shaped much of the Catholic immigrant population for two centuries.[22] Type D (Distant God) suggests the description of God that emerged from the American Enlightenment and the deist movement at the turn of

17. Ibid., 34.

18. Ibid., 31–34.

19. Ibid., 33.

20. Ibid., 32.

21. See further George M. Marsden, *Fundamentalism and American Culture: The Shaping of Twentieth Century Evangelicalism, 1870–1925* (New York: Oxford University Press, 1980).

22. See further Thomas F. O'Meara, *Fundamentalism: A Catholic Perspective* (Mahwah, NJ: Paulist Press, 1990), 21–35.

the nineteenth century has continued forward in various forms in the popular culture as well as in some churches.[23] Type B (Benevolent God) suggests the influence of American romantic and transcendental philosophy in the nineteenth century as well as the revival of some Catholic and Protestant understandings of sacramental theology in the wake of post–World War II renewal movements culminating in Vatican II.

Whatever the genesis of these dominant beliefs, the Baylor Religion Survey demonstrates that Americans' views fundamentally differ from the God of religious insight and Christian conversion. When a person enters into the process of religious insight within a Christian community that is fundamentally disoriented about the God of Jesus Christ, the inevitable result will be a diminished capacity of the individual to discover the God who interacts with him or her. This does not mean that genuine religious conversion is not possible but, rather, that it will often be skewed toward false gods.

From an authentically Christian perspective, the most important task facing those who advocate a wider theology of conversion is to reveal the God of Jesus Christ, not merely the gods of American popular culture. Someone who, in seeking that revelation, does embark upon the process of religious insight may come to discern fundamental differences from the dominant ethos. Recognizing the radical discrepancy between the conventional piety of most Christian communities and their own religious insight may cause them to feel like insider/outsiders: people who simultaneously find themselves fully steeped in the conventional ethos while having "new eyes and new ears" to see the world in radically different ways than they have been led to believe.

FALSE GODS IN AMERICAN CULTURE

From a Christian perspective, exposing the limited or "false" gods that obscure the divine life really present in human history is necessary for people who want to achieve the deepest levels of religious insight and

---

23. For further explanation of the evolution of the American Enlightenment, see Donald L. Gelpi, *Varieties of Transcedental Experience: A Study in Constructive Postmodernism* (Collegeville, MN: Liturgical Press, 2000), 3–84.

holistic adult conversion. Viewed from a Christian perspective, four different categories of false gods can be identified in America: the Authoritarian, the Benevolent, the Critical, and the Distant.

Authoritarian God

The most dangerous type of God from a Christian perspective is the type of Authoritarian God that actually is thought to be angriest at and even hate certain groups of people.

The God of anger and hate has been popular throughout history, and there is a long list of people he is thought to have hated over the ages. In recent times this type of God is often manifest in popular Christian political discourse on (ostensibly) Christian radio talk shows and cable news programs. This God's anger just happens to be directed toward the same people that represent the political opponents of certain socioeconomic and political forces. This is the God who tells people to only worry about themselves and their family, ethnic group, or nation, and insinuates that Christians have no responsibility for people who are different from them. This God is often thought to be most angry at those who seem to infringe on the "sacred way of life" of certain classes of people in the United States: this petty and defensive God seems to be threatened by the poor, undocumented immigrants, racial and ethnic minorities, people in developing countries, and homosexuals.

Benevolent God

It seems that American Christians often believe in two different types of a Benevolent God: the god of the consumer culture and the God who is like Santa Claus.

The God of the Consumer Culture. The God of the consumer culture is one that can be bought and sold like any other product or commodity. This is a God who simply wants what the believer wants. This God seems to have no plans or purposes and simply wants to make people happy, no matter how self-centered and unrealistic this happiness turns out to be. Believing in this God requires no pain, no sacrifices, and no worries about other people, bigger problems, and long-term plans. This is a God who never gets angry at injustice or impatient with the market forces and economic realities that allow so much inequity and poverty in the world. This God simply keeps people from worrying too much about the future or the bigger picture.

The God Who Is Like Santa Claus. Children often cannot tell the difference between God and Santa Claus. Both are imagined to be kindly old men with white beards who live in a far off place but "know if we've been bad or good." This is the God who is like Santa Claus to whom believers simply give a list of their needs and who comes occasionally to give them rewards and presents. Many people worship this God on Sunday in the hope that if they do their part, he will do his part and give them what they need (or want). As children get older they quit believing in Santa Claus because they discover that other people actually give them what they want, or they just learn to get it for themselves. They eventually discover that just as Santa Claus is not real, neither is the God that they believe in. At this point, the Benevolent God is often seen as a type of childish belief that while comforting and benign, offers no real answer to the practical problems of daily life.

Critical God

The Critical God for Christians in the American culture seems to be primarily understood as a God who is the tough and demanding judge. This is the God whom many people feared as children and who still scares them even though they don't often admit it. This is the God who is sitting "up there" in judgment of them and whom they will have to face in the end. This God does not really like people or care for them and is only putting up with them because *he* is God and that's his job. Actually, this God is angry with people and intends to punish them for all the crazy things, silly mistakes, and mean acts that they have ever committed. This God has no patience with human failings and will not really care to hear our side of the story. This God will cut people off in midsentence and tell them to quit whining about their problems. Furthermore, people suspect that this God actually sends trials, temptations, frustrations, and crises to test them and even trip them up. This God seems to want people to fail; and when they don't live up to his unfair expectations, he will judge harshly, although he knew that people would never succeed in the first place.

Distant God

Many Americans generally seem to believe in a distant God who is seen in the light of technology and science. This is a disinterested God, a God who gets everything started, like a computer programmer, but then simply stands by and watches as the program unfolds. This God is simply watching us "from a distance," in the words of a popular song. This God may get involved to fix a few glitches in the system, but it is not clear why this God fixes some and ignores others. Praying to this God is like sending an e-mail to which we may or may not receive a response. By and large, this God is too busy or too powerless to care about or help us. This God doesn't hate or punish people; rather, the work here is basically done, and this God has moved on to other divine projects. Life just has to play itself out, and not even God can do much about it.

THE GOD OF JESUS CHRIST

The Personality of God in the New Testament

The God of Jesus Christ—that is the image of God that emerges from the teachings of Jesus in the Christian scriptures—stands in contradistinction to the "false gods" listed previously. The "personality" of this God is worth exploring. The Gospels report Jesus describing the God he experiences and represents in his life and ministry in five fundamental ways.[24]

God as "Abba." On a number of occasions, Jesus refers to God in a very intimate and personal way, literally as "daddy" or "papa."[25] Jesus even instructs his followers to imitate him in praying to God this way (Mk 14:36; Mt 6:9–13, 11:25, 12:50, 26:39; Lk 11:1–4, 22:42, 23:34, 46). This implies that God is never distant, impersonal,

---

24. I am deeply indebted to Thomas O'Meara for his insights about Jesus' view of God, primarily gleaned from my many interactions with him over the years. His clearest articulation of these insights can be found in his book *Theology of Ministry, Revised Edition* (New York: Paulist Press, 1999), 35–79.

25. For a further exploration of this theme, see Donald Gelpi, *The Firstborn of Many: A Christology for Converting Christians*, vol. 1 (Milwaukee: Marquette University Press, 2001), 300–301.

and unconnected. The God Jesus proclaims is intimately close to ordinary people, closer than the relationship of parent to child. People can no more be without God than they can be without a biological father and mother, in Jesus' view (Rom 8:14–17). Furthermore, the affectionate name implies that God not only loves humans in some kind of vague general way but also loves each person personally. It even implies that humans are pleasing to God and are meant to imitate God in their own lives (Lk 6:36–38).

God as Plan/Providence. For Jesus, God not only loves people as individuals but also knows and cares about each individual (Mt 6:25–34), God is working in each person's life to make it as rich and full as possible (Lk 4:6–21). Jesus makes it clear that although God gives humans control of the world and their lives, God does not abandon his creatures. Rather, considering us as children, God has a plan and intention for each person and is constantly working to help realize this plan as fully as possible (Eph 1:9). In Jesus' view human life is not an obstacle course. Each life is a project, with many possibilities, one of which is the choice to completely trust in the power of God. Jesus assures his followers that the real God is one whom can be completely and unconditionally trusted to bring about the fullest life possible for people who desire it (Jn 17:15–26).

God's Presence Is Everywhere. Jesus insists that God's presence and love is not confined to any one place, people, or religion (Jn 3:8, 16–18, 4: 21–24). After his Resurrection, Jesus' disciples realize that God is present to all people at all times in a number of different ways. One such way that God is present to people is through religious activities (worship, observances, etc.), but this does not exhaust God's activity. In fact, the normal arena of God's activity in the world is in and through each person's daily life. People primarily experience God's presence and respond to this presence through one's daily activities, one's relationships with others, and in the mundane events that make up day-to-day life.

God in Others. Jesus continually affirms that God's presence in the world is most direct and concrete in people (Mt 5:1–10, 25:31–46; 1 Jn 4:20–21). This implies that God is primarily present in each person. Furthermore, Jesus asserts that God's presence is most fully realized in the poor, the outcast, the suffering, in all of those who seem to society to be farthest away from God's love and attention. God can also be most present in a people's lives precisely when they find themselves included in one of these groups.

God as Compassion. Jesus proclaims through his words and actions that God "suffers with" humans (Lk 6:36–38). God, through Jesus, dwells and lives with people and allows himself to experience what they experience. For Christian believers, Jesus Christ, as God's concrete presence in the world as a human signifies that God practices what God preaches: love and absolute trust in the power of this love to fulfill human lives. God understood in the light of Jesus' life and proclamation leads to some insights about many of the limited and false understandings of God in American culture.

Implications of Jesus' View of God

In his letter to the Colossians, the apostle Paul claims that Jesus is "the image of the invisible God" (Col 1:15). Paul believed that Jesus, through his life and ministry, offered humanity a new understanding of the God who was the creator and sustainer of all life, an understanding that called into question views previously perceived as orthodox, even by Paul. Jesus' life and message challenged views of God commonly held by both the Jews and the Gentiles, offering both new interpretations of God's personality and intentions. Jesus' view of God continues to challenge people, even Christians, to reassess, alter, and change their understanding of God. Aspects of Jesus' view of God, as well as some implications of his life and message for Christians, are examined in the following.

The God of Jesus Christ Does Not Hate

This God does not judge people the way the world judges them. This God chooses the weak and the powerless, has a preferential concern for the poor, sinners, and those whom others deem unwelcome or unworthy. In Jesus, whom Christian theology traditionally understands as God incarnate, this God allowed himself to be labeled as a threat to society and its values, and to be executed as a common criminal, because he loved the "wrong" people. According to the Christian scriptures, Jesus reminds his followers that salvation is not finally about having the right ideas or belonging to the right group, or church, or class, or nation. Rather, it is about accepting the real presence of God in other people.

The God of Jesus Christ Cannot Be Bought and Sold

This God does not offer people temporary and superficial comforts but eternal divine life. Eternal life requires individuals to change and grow in ways that they cannot imagine and may not like. Christians, however, accept sacrifice, pain, and sorrow because they believe that some greater and more important future awaits those who trust God. Jesus' Resurrection gives Christians hope of personal resurrection and helps people to understand that the fullness of life—genuine happiness—can never be attained in this world.

The God of Jesus Christ Is Not Disinterested, Distant, or Powerless

The God that Jesus proclaims not only created the world but also has a plan for this world and all who live in it. This God intends to carry out the plan (called the "reign of God" by Jesus), but part of God's will includes human participation in that plan. Christians believe that God chose humans to cooperate with the divine will and to join God in bringing about the plan. Humans seem so inadequate and unhelpful, but God chose them and puts responsibility into their hands anyway. And Jesus leaves no doubt about his conviction that God's plans can and will be achieved. The only question has to do with the willingness of individuals to participate in the process. People can stall or subvert these plans if they choose, or they can advance and develop the divine process. In this view, human prayers are not just "shots in the dark" but a special kind of participation in the plan of God. God, as understood by Christians, expects people to pray, to ask for what they need, and to place their fears and anxieties about this world in God's hands. This is not done out of a sense of desperation, but in the firm belief that God is listening and will respond.

The God of Jesus Christ Became a Human Person

Christians believe that in the fullness of time God chose to reveal Godself and God's plan for the world through a human person. In this view, God did not send the world an idea, or a theory, or a list of rules to follow but a person: "The Word became flesh." This is God's ultimate revelation. Belief in this act makes Christianity unique. It also draws the line between authentic Christian doctrine and heresy. Most of the dominant forms of heresy throughout church history have tended to deny the genuine humanity of Christ: Gnosticism, Docetism, Manicheism, Albingensianism, Jansenism, and modern forms of fundamentalism all tend to deny or diminish the reality of Jesus' humanity.[26] Such denial diminishes the value of all humanity and history as well. Authentic Christian tradition believes that God sent a divine human person but someone with a body that functioned just like everyone else's—a body that needed food and water and shelter, had limited language skills, and had emotions, desires, and dysfunctions. This person learned primarily through imitation, just as all humans learn primarily through a complex process of imitation and interpretation. That people learn in this way may be the reason that God chose to send a person rather than an idea or a rule: Jesus teaches his followers and they teach one another how to be divine.

A truly incarnational Christianity understands salvation as a process of becoming a certain kind of person rather than holding particular ideas. In this view, one becomes divine by imitating the divine/human person of Jesus Christ in one's life. Christians view such imitation as possible only through the power of the Holy Spirit working in each person, "conforming" one to the image of Christ. Ideas, theories, and rules help people to interpret their lives properly, but they do not replace Jesus Christ, the enfleshed Word who cannot be fully understood in mere words.

Jesus may need to be rendered present in a new way if authentic Christianity is to thrive in the United States. In US culture, perhaps Christians cannot be overly incarnational in their approach to Christianity. The Incarnation is meant to serve as a tangible possibility for each human life. For Christians the Incarnation explains the inherent dignity of every human: it narrates the story of birth, the struggle

---

26. For a short summary of these heresies, see *Catechism of the Catholic Church* (Washington, DC: US Catholic Conference, *Libreria Editrice Vaticana*, 1994), nos. 115–121, and Elizabeth A Johnson, *Consider Jesus* (New York: Crossroad, 2002), 19–34.

for identity, purpose, and mission, the confrontation with sin, the limitations of death, and the response of God to this process (that is, resurrection). The Incarnation, understood as a divine person living the human experience, can offer hope to people living in a culture in which the dominant ideologies undervalue, discard, or invalidate the experience of most humans.

The God of Jesus Christ Creates, Sustains, and Is Revealed in a Community

To live as a community requires self-sacrifice and the willingness to commit oneself intelligently and critically to a long tradition and shared style of life. According to Christian sources, the God of Jesus Christ asked his followers to become his body: to live in a shared, interdependent manner of life that actually imitates the reality of God's own presence to the world. Jesus tells his followers that they will not find God on their own, neither will they normally experience the ongoing presence, love, and action of God in isolation from other people in some kind of private mystical vision. At the heart of Christianity is the conviction that God acts through people and that God calls people to respond to this action in their lives by treating other people as God wants them to be treated. By the sharing of gifts, resources, time, hearts, and minds with other people in an ongoing, mutually sustaining, and selfless way, humans can discover and represent the living presence of God in human history and in their own lives.

The God of Jesus Christ Created the Christian Community

Fundamental to Christian belief is that God loves the world so much that God remained faithful to the promise of salvation even after the world rejected the very Son of God—Jesus of Nazareth. Christians believe that in raising Jesus Christ to new life, the Creator sent the Holy Spirit—Jesus' own Spirit—upon his followers that they might all live as God intended and continue the saving mission and ministry of Jesus Christ throughout history. Christians believe that each person baptized in Christ's death and Resurrection receives a share of his own Spirit and a part of his mission. All the baptized together make up the body of Christ, and through the sharing of their unique gifts they all together mediate God's presence to the world. Every member of the body has an essential role to play in God's plan, and all the members share equally in the Spirit of Christ. Within the body there are many, many different functions, one of which is to lead the rest of the body in service to the world. Leadership in the body of Christ, like all forms of discipleship, is modeled after Jesus' ministry. This means that it is orientated completely toward love and service to others. Leadership means that one has a special responsibility but not a greater share in the Spirit. Gifts and responsibilities may differ, but there is only one Spirit given to all through the power of Jesus Christ and the sacramental power of baptism. Grace does not trickle down on us but is poured out freely on each person and, indeed, on the world through the one life and death of the Son of God and the radical gift of his Spirit.

The God of Jesus Christ Is Present in Compassionate Service

Jesus desired all to be one, united together in loving service to God. The example of Jesus' own life and death reminds Christians that other people are the presence of God in their lives and how believers treat them is how they treat God. Jesus insists that Christians, in the end, will take only the memory of who and how they have loved with them into the next life (Mt 25:31–46). The Christian God is the God of love, not hate. Moreover, faith calls all to live lives of radical and atoning acts of selfless love and to withhold all judgment and act solely out of love and compassion for everyone— even one's enemies.

CONCLUSION

Religious conversion does not necessarily mean Christian conversion, and even a Christian conversion is profoundly shaped by the cultural context in which it occurs. In the United States, where Christianity is splintered into numerous factions and denominations representing a whole myriad of possible interpretations of the gospel, it is not surprising that there is a crisis in Christianity. Even in a country where almost everyone believes in God, it is abundantly clear that not everyone believes in the same God, even when they share the same denominational affiliation. The challenge of Christian evangelization in this culture is the challenge of helping converted Christians to understand not just the gospel but also the practical implications of the reign of God for their lives. According to Christian belief, being converted to the God of Jesus Christ puts one in a relationship with a radically loving and caring God who demonstrates the depth of his love through entering into our human condition and sharing in all aspects of human life. This radical love does not diminish God but sanctifies human life and raises it up to share in a divine destiny. In the Christian view, God becomes human so that humans can become divine. Christians believe that those who truly affirm this fundamental belief about God and humanity will be changed in ways that move beyond mere piety and religious practice; it will set them on a journey to change the world. Believing in the God of Jesus Christ joins the individual to a community of believers who are united by Christ's own Spirit to work for the coming of the reign of God that he preached. Christians see this journey of universal and even cosmic transformation as the ultimate practical implication of Christian conversion.

QUESTIONS FOR REFLECTION

1. Are you surprised by the statistics about religious belief in the US culture as reported by the various polls cited? Does the information in these polls conform to your experience of the belief among your family and friends?

2. Which understanding of God discussed in the Baylor Religion Survey is most pervasive in US culture, in your view?

3. Articulate the differences between James and Royce on the nature of religious experience? What difference does each of their views make for understanding spirituality and religion? Which views are most convincing?

4. Do you agree that there are "false gods" in US culture? If so, what are the negative effects of these false understandings of God?

5. Do you find any aspects of the understanding of God revealed by Jesus Christ to be surprising or confusing? Explain.

6. How does one's view of God shape one's religious conversion? Alternatively, how does one's religious conversion shape one's view of God? Is a person's view of God shaped by one's level of affective, intellectual, moral, and sociopolitical conversion? Explain. Does one's view of God limit the possibility of non-religious conversion? Why or why not?

FOR FURTHER READING

Augustine of Hippo, *The Confessions and Enchiridion*, trans. and ed. Albert Outler (Grand Rapids, MI: Christian Classics Ethereal Library, 1955).

Cone, James, *God of the Oppressed*, Revised Edition (Maryknoll, NY: Orbis Press, 1997).

Day, Dorothy, *The Long Loneliness* (San Francisco: Harper and Row, 1952).

James, William, *The Varieties of Religious Experience* (New York: New American Library, 1958). Published from the Gifford Lectures of 1901–1902.

Johnson, Elizabeth A., *Consider Jesus* (New York: Crossroad, 2002).

———. *Quest for the Living God: Mapping Frontiers in the Theology of God* (New York: Continuum, 2007).

Lash, Nicholas, *Easter in Ordinary: Reflections on Human Experience and the Knowledge of God* (Notre Dame, IN: University of Notre Dame Press, 1990).

Marsden, George M., *Fundamentalism and American Culture: The Shaping of Twentieth-Century Evangelicalism, 1870–1925* (New York: Oxford University Press, 1980).

Nolan, Albert, *Jesus Before Christianity*, Revised Edition (Maryknoll, NY: Orbis Press, 1992).

Noll, Mark A., *America's God* (London: Oxford University Press, 2002).

O'Meara, Thomas, *Fundamentalism: A Catholic Perspective* (Mahwah, NJ: Paulist Press, 1990).

Proudfoot, Wayne, *Religious Experience* (Berkeley: University of California Press, 1987).

Putnam, Robert D., and David E. Campbell, *American Grace: How Religion Divides and Unites Us* (New York: Simon and Schuster, 2010).

Royce, Josiah, *The Sources of Religious Insight* (New York: Charles Scribner's Sons, 1912).

Taylor, Charles, *Varieties of Religion Today: William James Revisited, Institute for Human Sciences Vienna Lectures* (Boston: Harvard University Press, 2003).

Wright, N. T., *How God Became King: The Forgotten Story of the Gospels* (New York: HarperOne, 2012).

———. *The Challenge of Jesus* (London: Society for Promoting Christian Knowledge, 2000).

———. *Paul and the Faithfulness of God* (Minneapolis, MN: Fortress Press, 2013).

7

Authenticating Christian Conversion
The Option for the Poor

We love because he first loved us. Those who say, "I love God," and hate their brothers and sisters, are liars; for those who do not love a brother or sister whom they have seen, cannot love God whom they have not seen. The commandment we have from him is this: those who love God must love their brothers and sisters also.

—1 John 4:19–21

CHRISTIAN SPIRITUALITY AND EMPATHY

To be a part of an ongoing communal conversion experience, one must become aware of how the words and actions of one member affect those of another. Humans learn empathy—seeing reality from another person's perspective—and deepen their empathy when as members of a community; they grapple with situations that extend them beyond their immediate boundaries. Because empathy presumes that people view the world mysteriously, it is attuned to the complexity of every situation and the possibility that things are not as they immediately or obviously seem. Empathy challenges one's perceptions of the status quo, allowing each person to remain open to the possibility—even probability—that nuances and distinctions will be revealed that change his or her view of the situation, of reality.

Empathy is essential to ongoing conversion. In the biblical story, Moses, having been raised by his sister and mother (Ex 2:7–10), must have been profoundly sensitized to the ways of the Hebrew people to the struggles of their daily lives. This sense of empathy for their condition, must have deeply affected Moses even after he was returned to pharaoh's daughter and came to his full maturity in pharaoh's house.

By sensitizing people to the myriad other possible interpretations of human experience, genuine empathy displaces one from the comfort of an established worldview that is the hallmark of any social ethos. This displacement not only causes personal discomfort and psychological uncertainty, it also literally draws one out of the established ethos. Empathy makes people feel like outsiders because it causes them to challenge the common assumptions of their social system and because it moves them to identify with others who perceive their social system as a threat or a danger to their very lives.

Empathy also gives humans the capacity to imagine the world differently. Once displaced from their conventional ethos—when they begin to look at it as outsiders—they can hope and believe that the world could be different in very concrete and practical ways. Enabling individuals to expand their fundamental life commitments beyond their own socioeconomic and ethnic milieu, empathy calls them into commitment with communities that may be suffering and into solidarity with causes greater than themselves. When empathy is generalized, it becomes true solidarity, the most positive antidote to radical individualism. In addition, the vision and commitment of true solidarity create the conditions for genuine hopefulness to dispel the chronic despair of the US ethos.

REAL POVERTY VS. SPIRITUAL POVERTY

As stated in chapter 3, the ideology of free-market capitalism serves as a tremendous force at the center of the global economy. Free-market capitalism acts as a massive catalyst for creating wealth, providing jobs, developing resources, and advancing technology at unprecedented levels throughout the world. There is no doubt that this economic system rewards risk, innovation, efficiency, and hard work with dramatic profits. Likewise, it often succeeds at providing goods and services to an ever-larger percentage of the world's population. Consequently, it is easy to understand the widely held belief in the possibilities of free-market capitalism to transform the world in a positive way.

While true that free-market capitalism works as a giant engine for creating wealth and distributing goods and services worldwide, it also creates "winners" and "losers" in the process. It does generate incredible wealth, but it does not distribute that wealth equitably. As Karl Polanyi demonstrates, capitalism tends to amass wealth in the hands of a small percentage of the population it serves, while at the same time diminishing resources at unimaginable and unreplenishable rates.[1] Its success and efficiency often come as the result of reducing humans and their labor to commodities that can be bought and sold, used and discarded, leveraged and withheld, without any concern for the consequences of this process on the humans who have been commodified.

The winners at the top of this economic pyramid find themselves accumulating wealth and resources (and also needing still more wealth and resources) at an almost dizzying pace. Similarly, those at the bottom of this economic system find themselves actually loosing what little economic and social stability they had managed to achieve, often becoming completely engulfed in seemingly endless cycles of deprivation and poverty. Free-market capitalism depends on an ideology that relegates a staggering percentage of the world's population to the losing side of its ideological equation. One must acknowledge both the success of free-market capitalism and the condition of economic injustice, human suffering, and social disintegration that it creates and sustains. For persons at the top of the economic system to recognize the presence in the world of the poor requires that they acknowledge some complicity in and dependence on their condition.

In the Christian tradition, the solidarity that signifies integral adult conversion is identified with the preferential option for the poor as an organizing principle and a concrete test of conversion. In Christ, one realizes that his or her true destiny is with the children of Abraham (Heb 11:24–26). In the biblical account, Jesus completely

1. Karl Polanyi, *The Great Transformation: The Political and Economic Origins of Our Time* (Boston: Beacon Press, 1957), 141–70, 187–200.

identified with the poor, sick, and outcasts in a way that led to his execution, so any attempt to imitate Christ in unity with his Spirit must necessarily include this radical identification with the marginalized members of society. Jesus made it clear that the beloved community would rectify unjust social orders: "The last will be first, and the first will be last" (Mt 20:16). Christians associate salvation with recognizing the plight of the poor and working actively to alleviate their suffering and give to them in their need.[2]

The renowned liberation theologian Gustavo Gutiérrez emphatically asserts "poverty means *death*."[3] Gutiérrez defends this assertion by analyzing the reality of poverty:

> Food shortages, housing shortages, the impossibility of attending properly to health and educational needs, the exploitation of labor, chronic unemployment, disrespect for human worth and dignity, unjust restrictions on freedom of expression (in politics and religion alike) are the daily plight of the poor. The lot of the poor, in a word, is suffering. Theirs is a situation that destroys peoples, families, and individuals.[4]

The primary condition of the impoverished is scarcity; those who are poor constantly lack the basic necessities of life; daily, they face the possibility of the loss of life for themselves and their families. This constant presence of death is the most ominous and destructive dimension of poverty.

Gutiérrez also insists that "to be poor is a way of life."[5] This means that poverty creates ways of thinking, loving, praying, eating, celebrating, viewing the past and future, raising children, and living together in family and community that transcend mere survival. To be poor also aligns one with the struggle for justice, peace, and liberty. The poor are not merely condemned to passive acceptance but

---

2. See Daniel Groody, *Globalization, Spirituality, and Justice* (Maryknoll, NY: Orbis Books, 2007), 194–202.

3. Gustavo Gutiérrez, "Option for the Poor," in *Mysterium Liberationis*, ed. Ignacio Ellacuria and Jon Sobrino (Maryknoll, NY: Orbis, 1993), 236.

4. Ibid.

5. Ibid.

are increasingly confronting the oppressive structures that face them. Poverty as a way of life resists the constant presence of death through an active appropriation of those dimensions of life that cannot be directed or controlled by inhuman structures and outside forces.

Pointing to the document adopted at Medellín by the Latin American bishops in 1968 titled "Document on Poverty," Gutiérrez posits a distinction between three types of poverty: real poverty, as an evil (that is, not desired by God); spiritual poverty, as availability to the will of God; and solidarity with the poor, as well as the situation they suffer.[6] In this particular moment in history, he explains, there has been an "irruption" of real poverty to the extent that it constitutes a crisis that cries for the immediate and direct attention of both the church and the secular world.

According to Gutiérrez, real poverty and God's preferential commitment does not imply exclusivity but, rather, points to those who must be the first (consciously, temporally, existentially) to be served by the healing and reconciling power of the new life offered by Christ's resurrection and by those who have been filled with Christ's Spirit to carry on his saving mission. The preferential option for the poor is an immediate and morally binding sense of solidarity with the real poor, a commitment that leads to a sense of spiritual poverty that, in turn, opens the person to do whatever God asks on behalf of the poor. In this sense, the preferential option for the poor unites the whole Christian community in a single vision that is both profoundly practical (in that its direct object is the elimination of real poverty in all its manifestations) and universally transcendent (in that it represents the highest goal of the beloved community, which can only be fully achieved in the eschaton, the new and heavenly Jerusalem of Revelation 21).

The preferential option for the poor, therefore, serves as the cause that underlies a morally coherent Christian life. Furthermore, far from excluding other causes or being the exclusive domain of Christians or even religious persons, this cause transcends boundaries of belief and ideology, just as the crisis of real poverty does. The preferential option for the poor would find common cause with any community of truly devoted individuals who seek to relieve

---

6. Ibid., 235.

suffering and oppression, discrimination and injustice, inhumanity and dehumanizing conditions in any manner in which they occur in any society or culture. The option for the poor offers a vision of a community united despite cultural, religious, socioeconomic, and political boundaries, a community that fulfills the Pauline vision and genuinely saves all those who participate in it at any level or in any authentic and fully committed way.

THANKSGIVING AS A FOUNDATION MYTH

The conditions of scarcity and violence that create real poverty are present in the United States. Their presence, however, is not pervasive throughout the general population; in fact, the majority of the most recent generation of Americans has seldom experienced real poverty. Many factors prevent the occurrence of life-threatening shortages in America. Americans proclaim freedom from the conditions of real poverty in many ways, most evidently in common modes of celebrating the holiday of Thanksgiving.

Thanksgiving is not just a national holiday; it is an educational event forming the common consciousness of the American people. Because Thanksgiving is observed in virtually the same way across socioeconomic, racial, religious, and ethnic lines, it creates a common experience that informs the imagination and memory of most Americans. Like any traditional feast, Thanksgiving functions as an opportunity to gather family and friends for celebration and conversation. At another level, however, it teaches and reinforces a fundamental aspect of the dominant cultural mythos. The Thanksgiving myth shapes the way individual Americans think of their country and its story, but it gives form to each American's personal story and destiny as well.

The Thanksgiving story is a foundation myth because it is largely removed from any actual historical events and instead has emerged as a central ritualized event in American culture. A "foundation myth" is a sociological concept of a narrative that both describes how a society or group came into being and also offers some insight into the way that the group does or should understand itself. Understood thus, Thanksgiving is a myth not so much because modern observance has only a tenuous connection to actual history (although that is the case), but because it *functions* as a foundation myth for society. In other words, while it is based on some real incidents in the early history of the European colonization of the North American continent, it eventually becomes formalized in a way that helps fit a wider view of the American experience. Thanksgiving symbolizes the broader American narrative: the first settlers' realization of the blessing that the new continent represents and the understanding that the whole community needs to be grateful to God for bringing them into this exceptional land. Thanksgiving functions as a way of identifying the United States with the "promised land" that God gave to the Hebrew people after their rescue from slavery in Egypt. The concept of America as the new Promised Land, a land filled with milk and honey, lies at the heart of even the most secularized understanding of the Thanksgiving myth. America is understood as a land of abundance with a divine mandate. This is what gives Thanksgiving the character of a profoundly sacred and fundamental ritual in American life.

Thanksgiving offers Americans an opportunity to appreciate all the blessings they have received from the Almighty or, in more secular terms, to contemplate the abundant resources for life and happiness that are available to both individuals and the nation as a whole. The communal dimension of Thanksgiving expresses itself in the belief that the United States as a nation has been blessed with an abundance of resources, wealth, and liberty. This abundance, though not shared equally among all citizens, nevertheless, grounds the American dream and serves as a common reserve from which the whole nation draws, and all citizens can aspire to a greater share. At Thanksgiving, Americans remember not only the blessings of abundance but also recall this abundance as a sign of the special role in world history that God has destined for this nation.

The problem with this American myth is that American abundance often depends directly on a scarcity of resources, wealth, and liberty in many other parts of the world.[7] Because of the tendency of the free-market economy to create winners *and losers*, the belief that God has particularly blessed America (i.e., to make them winners)

---

7. The tendency of free-market economies to produce abundance for some of the impoverishment of others was discussed at some length in chapter 3.

implies that God has chosen to do so at the expense of the poor and outcasts in much of the rest of globe (i.e., to make them losers). The good life that American abundance represents directly causes scarcity that means real poverty and that leads to death in many parts of the world. The situation creates an obvious dialectic: either God has chosen to make America wealthy at the expense of the poor or the myth of American exceptionalism—the idea that God has uniquely chosen America for special blessing—is false.

This dialectic does not go totally unnoticed in American culture. The common response to it, however, is to donate out of our abundant money and other resources to partially alleviate the immense suffering in the rest of the world. American donations are not insignificant, but they are ultimately inadequate to solve the fundamental problem of scarcity that exists in many countries. Therefore, we Americans are left in a quandary as to how to help the impoverished while maintaining the lifestyle that the American dream requires. From a Christian perspective, of course, one cannot maintain this dialectic through any form of generosity or charity. When abundance *requires* scarcity, the system is inherently unworkable and needs to be changed. To simply give from one's abundance, while it may have some moral value, does nothing to address the underlying systemic problem that only a systemic reorientation of the global distribution of goods can address. The problem Americans face is not one of insufficient charity but a seeming unwillingness to face the basic injustice inherent in the economic system that produces American prosperity and abundance.

An alternative account of the Thanksgiving myth can be imagined. This version of the myth, like the current Thanksgiving myth, is a selective retelling of actual history but has the virtue of offering a healthier foundation myth for American society. The original settlement at Plymouth Colony was on the verge of famine and total collapse until Wampanoag Indians, the native people of the region, intervened.[8] These indigenous people were able to help the pilgrims adapt to the conditions of the new continent as well as understand the fundamental principles that governed people who had lived on

---

8. See further Elizabeth Armstrong, "The First Thanksgiving," *The Christian Science Monitor* (November 27, 2002).

this land for centuries. These principles seemed to have been based more on the desire to create a subsistent environment for all than on an abundance/scarcity dialectic. By sharing their knowledge and resources with the colonists, the native people literally saved the pilgrims from death without diminishing their own lives.

In this narrative, Thanksgiving becomes a celebration of the fundamental gift of life and the opportunity for all to recommit knowledge and resources in a way that all have life. Rather than reinforcing the myth of abundance, this Thanksgiving narrative calls Americans to desire instead to develop a system of international cooperation that would ensure that all people share the basic promise of life and human dignity—as justice requires. This economy, which aims at producing subsistence, would be radically different from the economic system of the American dream, which aims at producing nearly unlimited abundance.

It is, of course, not at all clear that most Americans, even Christian Americans, are ready to gratefully embrace the level of change (conversion) that a subsistence-promoting system would require.

THE PREFERENTIAL OPTION FOR THE POOR IS AT THE HEART OF CHRISTIAN LIFE

The Christian term *Eucharist* is a Greek word meaning "thanksgiving."[9] For Christians, the fundamental story that is the source of their gratitude is the story of Jesus offering his own life in proclamation of the beloved community. The life, death, and Resurrection of Jesus serve as the organizing matrix around which the gospel message is organized.

As already noted, the beloved community of Jesus' vision will be characterized by a special concern for the poor, marginalized, and despised members of society. While no one is excluded from this

---

9. See further Josef Andreas Junmann, "Eucharist," in *Encyclopedia of Theology: The Concise Sacramentum Mundi*, ed. Karl Rahner (New York: Seabury Press, 1975), 447–67; David N. Power, *The Eucharistic Mystery: Revitalizing the Tradition* (New York: Crossroads, 1992); and Jerome Murphy-O'Connor, "Eucharist and Community in First Corinthians," in *Living Bread, Saving Cup*, ed. Kevin Seasoltz, (Collegeville, MN: Liturgical Press, 1982), 1–29.

reign in principle, Jesus asserted that many would choose to ignore it because it could not penetrate the shell that their privilege and wealth had created. Others would reject it outright and even resist it because it challenged the position of comfort and power that they had attained through the current order of things.

Jesus understood that those in positions of power and success in the social, political, and religious dimensions of society would not be happy to hear that these attainments would mean nothing in the beloved community. Jesus' message sounds like a call to revolution to them; rather than being good news, it threatens their whole way of life. For this reason those in power when Jesus was preaching in Jerusalem tried first to silence him, and ultimately resorted to killing him, as authorities had murdered so many of the prophets throughout the history of Israel. Jesus did not flee from them; instead, he confronted them more and more directly with his radical message. In the end, he publicly put all of his trust in God, whose plan he had come to fulfill. His willing acceptance of his execution was not an abdication to the power of the authorities but a profound act of refusal to accept their authority over his life.

Christians believe that Jesus' Resurrection confirmed the authority of Jesus' life and preaching and that by raising Jesus from the dead, God ratified the unique identity and ministry of Jesus in a dramatic and public way. God also definitively repudiated the principalities and powers of this world, demonstrating instead God's ultimate power over life and death. Furthermore, by sending the divine Spirit upon the communities of believers who witnessed the Resurrection, God empowered them to continue the ministry of Jesus and to immediately begin living as a beloved community. Following Jesus' example and the guidance of the Spirit, these communities explicitly rejected the idea that abundance and scarcity are acts of God, choosing instead to share all they had in common, in a subsistent way of living. The gift of the Spirit continues to animate the Christian community, ensuring that it will keep the message of the good news alive throughout time and will steadfastly proclaim the beloved community to all parts of the world.

Jesus, life, death, and Resurrection, and God's sending of the Holy Spirit are the foundations of Christian thanksgiving. The source of genuine Christian gratitude is the belief that God shares

God's own life with the poor and powerless, that new life comes from the willing acceptance of death, and that the beloved community serves as the only guiding vision for all social relationships.

The Christian Eucharist serves as an indictment of the fundamental injustice of all social and economic systems that dehumanize large parts of the population and do not ensure the basic human dignity of all people. In practice, this means that the Christian Eucharist will always challenge the dominant ideologies of the world and the economic systems that condemn so many people to real poverty. The celebration of the Eucharist has informed the imagination and memory of Christians throughout history. It should also shape the consciousness of American Christians so that they can identify more closely with the alternative Thanksgiving myth suggested in this chapter. The Eucharist aligns all aspects of Christian life with the abundant blessings that the beloved community represents for all humanity. The Eucharist also directly puts the preferential option for the poor at the heart of Christian life and worship. Because Jesus so intimately identified with the plight of the socially marginalized, no celebration of his victory can be complete without an explicit acknowledgment that conditions of inequality and suffering must be overturned. The Christian Eucharist sends the community forth to struggle against the principalities and powers and to transform this world.

Given this more complete understanding of the Christian message, one cannot have an integral Christian conversion and simply maintain life as usual. However, what does genuine empathy require? How can average Christians shape their own lives with an option for the poor? To put it in personal terms: does the option for the poor require a radical redistribution of an individual's resources and income and that of their families'?

LIVING IN GENUINE SOLIDARITY WITH THE POOR

The same is true with respect to the individual oppressor as person. Discovering himself to be an oppressor may cause considerable anguish, but it does not necessarily lead to solidarity with the oppressed. Rationalizing his guilt through paternalistic treatment of the oppressed, all the while holding them fast in a position of dependence, will not do. Solidarity requires that one enter into the situation of those with whom one is in solidarity; it is a radical posture. . . . true solidarity with the oppressed means fighting at their side to transform the objective reality which has made them these "beings for another." The oppressor is in solidarity with the oppressed only when he stops regarding the oppressed as an abstract category and sees them as persons who have been unjustly dealt with, deprived of their voice, cheated in the sale of their labor—when he stops making pious, sentimental, and individualistic gestures and risks an act of love. True solidarity is found only in the plenitude of this act of love, in its existentiality in its praxis. To affirm that men and women are persons and as persons should be free, and yet to do nothing tangible to make this affirmation a reality, is a farce.[10]

The passage quoted, from the groundbreaking work *The Pedagogy of the Oppressed* by Brazilian author Paulo Freire, concisely articulates the dilemma North Americans face. No individual, regardless of wealth, power, or international stature, can change the world's socioeconomic structures alone. It is not even clear that a large movement could successfully challenge the intricate system of inequality and injustice that defines global economics within a single generation or even over multiple generations. The viable path to a universal subsistence-producing economy remains unknown, and hopes for immediate, radical change are groundless. Nevertheless, the converted cannot put off the spiritual poverty that Christian conversion requires, neither can they await some widespread process before changing their own lives. While the hope for success comes not from a political or economic plan but Jesus' Resurrection, Christians must act immediately to alleviate suffering and oppression where it exists in any way possible. For Christians, the Resurrection

---

10. Paulo Freire, *Pedagogy of the Oppressed*, trans. Myra Bergman Ramos (New York: Continuum, 1970), 34–35.

serves as the absolute assurance that no good acts and no faithful response to the needs of the poor will go unnoticed or unfulfilled. In the Christian view, one's practical solidarity with the poor and the simple acts of love and justice it connotes will ultimately join with the Holy Spirit's acting to bring human history the goal that Jesus announced centuries ago.

Christian spirituality, as described above, offers a way out of the perplexing state in which most Americans find themselves. The preferential option for the poor is a way of coordinating a new and broader outlook that challenges the dominant ethos while also building on the significant strengths of the American character and tradition. Spiritualities rooted in the option for the poor can serve as modes of pedagogy (educative method) in conversion for those who find themselves trapped in the insular environment of privilege and wealth. Because this doctrine is first of all practical—it seeks to redress real poverty and oppression and death—it opens the way to draw on the most impressive achievement of American culture: its ability to find practical solutions to difficult problems.

Pragmatists by nature and social training, Americans drawn into small but interconnected communities devoted to solidarity with the poor can use their collective ingenuity to devise simple but effective methods of adapting to a subsistence model of living. By slowly but persistently discovering new and concrete ways to transform their lifestyles, these converted communities can begin to shape a genuine alternative to the free-market ethos. Such communities would offer hope to a world ensnared in poverty and the hopelessness it breeds. This hope would be the first and most significant fruit of any steps taken in solidarity.

Most traditional Christian spiritualities are based on the values of radical discipleship and community, not in place of personal growth and authenticity but as conditions necessary for full conversion. These spiritualities, thus, offer the very thing that American culture needs: a coherent vision that includes real solidarity while also leading to authentic personal fulfillment. Christian spirituality in the North American context, therefore, needs to be as much a process of recovery as invention.

It is helpful to reclaim some of the classic Christian spiritual traditions on their own terms. The major mendicant spiritualities

that originated in the High Middle Ages, for instance, were fundamentally founded to bring the church into an authentic relationship
with the materially poor and socially neglected members of emerging urban populations. These spiritualities provide a rich synthesis of
radical personal and communal poverty that attempts to bring about
genuine solidarity. Dominican, Franciscan, Carmelite, and Augustin-
ian spiritualities all combine an emphasis on active apostolate and
profound personal fidelity with a vibrant and varied communal life
and commitment.

Many of the most popular Christian mystics and spiritual writers in US culture—Francis of Assisi, Meister Eckhart, Catherine of
Siena, and Teresa of Avila—come out of this tradition. One cannot
adequately understand any of these authors outside of their communal and apostolic context; their interior spiritual journeys and the
experiences that they articulate are inherently connected to their
fundamental loyalty to community and gospel-based discipleship.
Contemporary American communities dedicated to solidarity and
subsistence could adapt many aspects of these spiritualities. Most
important, these authors, and the traditions out of which they
emerged, insist that the foundation of spiritual poverty and genuine
solidarity lies in an absolute faith in God's providential care: belief
in God's goodness and gracious intention to redeem all creation
grounds all virtuous moral acts and ethical decisions. Embracing
spiritual poverty requires that one believe at one's core that the
world has a meaning and purpose to which one can attune oneself and that some transcendent power exists to direct all moral and
sociopolitical commitment.

Communities experimenting with alternative and subsistent
modes of life will require members who are growing in all aspects
of conversion. Living in genuine solidarity with the poor will require
a sophisticated integration of moral, sociopolitical, and religious
conversions; it will also demand creative intellects open to dramatic
challenges and radical adaptations. Most of the Christian spiritual
schools developed modes of pedagogy to guide adults in the process of conversion. These formative pedagogies offer a foundation
upon which subsistent communities can build their own processes
of personal formation.

CONCLUSION

Integral adult conversion requires a dedication to some cause or purpose greater than one's own individual self-interest. This devotion to a higher cause and a community of those who work for this purpose acts as the litmus test of the extent of the transformation process. In the Christian tradition, the preferential option for the poor serves as a primary higher cause for all the converted. The option for the poor potentially integrates all the dimensions of adult conversion. Commitment to the cause of elimination of real poverty and creating the structures of justice and peace that ensure that all people live with the basic level of human dignity that they deserve denote the fullness of Christian conversion.

The belief that each person is called to a personal relationship with the divine life through the action of the Holy Spirit in human hearts grounds all forms of Christian spirituality. This implies that every human person can become attuned with actions of the divine in their lives and the wider world if that person responds to the offer of grace. Furthermore, Christian understandings of spirituality rest on the belief that one can only attune oneself to the actions of God in the world through a real empathy with the voice of the poor and oppressed of this world and through entering into some genuine form of solidarity with the poor in response to these voices. The response of individuals and communities to the voices of the poor authenticates Christian conversion, the spirituality that emerges from this conversion experience and the new way of living that this spirituality creates. Authentic Christian conversion then enables believers to teach and encourage others to open themselves to the full transformative power that this life offers.

For Christians the life, death, and Resurrection of Jesus Christ connote the foundational experience of a life truly lived in solidarity with the poor. Real poverty leads to death in a literal sense and in a myriad of ways. Jesus' fundamental identification with and care for the poor and outcasts of his world ensured that he would meet their fate in violence and death. In the Christian view, Jesus' Resurrection from the dead vindicates his absolute trust in the power and merciful intentions of the Father, and ensures that his example of empathy and solidarity would endure. Christians see the Resurrection as demonstrating Jesus' unique identification with the divine will and offering profound hope to all those who desire to imitate Jesus and continue his mission knowing that the consequences of this imitation could well be suffering and death. The Resurrection, in the Christian view, also enabled Jesus to share his divine Spirit with the whole community of believers that he gathered around him and that subsequently expanded throughout the world.

The fundamental problem in American culture lies in economic and sociopolitical structures that often make a genuine option for the poor untenable. Americans are engulfed in economic structures that are enmeshed in an abundance/scarcity dialectic that generates most of the real poverty in the world. For ordinary people, breaking free of this system presents a daunting, if not impossible, task. More important, the social and cultural realities in which Americans exist make it equally difficult to even see the truth about this situation. This prevailing social context tends to block a preferential option for the poor; therefore, the conditions for an integral and holistic Christian conversion are currently lacking in much of American society. This creates a practically intolerable situation not just for Christians but also for all the authentically converted.

The challenge then for American Christians is not to abandon their culture but to find ways to enable the kind of genuine empathy that draws people into a spiritual journey that leads one out of the enclave of the American ethos. This spiritual journey requires a community devoted to spiritual poverty and solidarity with the real poor throughout the world. It also requires a shared hope that all forms of genuine solidarity are ultimately joined to a universal and transcendent process of transformation that will prevail. For Christians, it is precisely the hope of the coming of reign of God as proclaimed by Jesus of Nazareth that empowers and energizes the community to move beyond paralysis and despair.

However, the question that all the converted must face is how to create the conditions that will aid this process of conversion in everyone. Ultimately, there is a need to offer others the tools that will enable them to enter into conversion in all dimensions of life. This means also that there is a need for a series of social structures and educational processes that encourage and enable openness, adaptation, and transformation from the start of life. This ultimately requires a new kind of pedagogy, a new approach to forming children and adults and a new lifestyle that encourages change, growth, and development in all dimensions of life. The converted must actively engage their social and cultural environment to create the conditions that make conversion possible and desirable. The creation of conditions necessary to produce affective, intellectual, moral, sociopolitical, and religious conversion is incumbent on all those who know that their true destiny lies outside the closed walls of American culture.

QUESTIONS FOR REFLECTION

1. How significant is a person's capacity for empathy in integral adult conversion as it has been explained in this text?
2. Is the preferential option for the poor an effective, relevant way to think about solutions to the problem of systematic injustice in the world? Why or why not?
3. Why does poverty mean death according to Gutiérrez? Does empathy with the poor require experience of poverty? Why or why not?
4. Is the preferential option for the poor consistent with the Judeo-Christian tradition as you understand it? Why or why not? Who are the poor referred to in the Hebrew and Christian scriptures? What besides material poverty constitutes being impoverished? Who in the United States in addition to the materially poor needs to be liberated?
5. What practical effects might result if the majority of US residents took the preferential option for the poor seriously?
6. How might the celebration of Thanksgiving in the United States enhance individuals' capacity for empathy for those who are poor and marginalized throughout the world?
7. Based on the discussion in this text, how does personal spirituality inform an understanding of real poverty versus spiritual poverty? To what extent does it integrate a preferential option of the poor?

FOR FURTHER READING

Boff, Leonardo, and Clodovis Boff, *Introducing Liberation Theology* (Maryknoll, NY: Orbis Press, 1987).

Bonino, José Míguez, *Toward a Christian Political Ethics* (Philadeplphia: Fortress Press, 1983).

Cone, James, *A Black Theology of Liberation* (Maryknoll, NY: Orbis Press, 1990).

Ellacuría, Ignacio, and Jon Sobrino, eds., *Mysterium Liberationis: Fundamental Concepts of Liberation Theology* (Maryknoll, NY: Orbis Press, 1993).

Freire, Paulo, *Pedagogy of Hope*, trans. Robert Barr (New York: Continuum, 2007).

———. *Pedagogy of the Oppressed*, trans. Myra Bergman Ramos (New York: Continuum, 1970).

Groody, Daniel G., *Globalization, Spirituality, and Justice* (Mayknoll, NY: Orbis, 2007).

Gutiérrez, Gustavo, *A Theology of Liberation: History,Politics, and Salvation* (Maryknoll, NY: Orbis Press, 1988).

Jungmann, Josef Andreas, SJ, "Eucharist," in *Encyclopedia of Theology: The Concise Sacramentum Mundi*, ed. Karl Rahner (New York: Seabury Press, 1975).

LaCugna, Catherine, ed., *Freeing Theology: The Essentials of Theology in a Feminist Perspective* (San Francisco: Harper, 1993).

Murphy-O'Connor, Jerome, "Eucharist and Community in First Corinthians," in *Living Bread, Saving Cup*, ed. Kevin Seasoltz (Collegeville, MN: Liturgical Press, 1982).

Phan, Peter, *Christianity with an Asian Face: Asian American Theology in the Making* (Maryknoll, NY: Orbis Press, 2003).

Power, David N., *The Eucharistic Mystery: Revitalizing the Tradition* (New York: Crossroads, 1992).

Rolheiser, Ronald, *Our One Great Act of Fidelity: Waiting for Christ in the Eucharist* (New York: Doubleday, 2011).

8

Dismantling the Walls of Pharaoh's House

> It is only the oppressed who, by freeing themselves, can free their oppressors. The latter, as an oppressive class, can free neither others nor themselves. It is therefore essential that the oppressed wage the struggle to resolve the contradiction in which they are caught; and the contradiction will be resolved by the appearance of the new man: neither oppressor nor oppressed, but man in the process of liberation. If the goal of the oppressed is to become fully human, they will not achieve their goal by merely reversing the terms of the contradiction, by simply changing poles.
>
> This may seem simplistic; it is not. Resolution of the oppressor-oppressed contradiction indeed implies the disappearance of the oppressors as a dominant class.
>
> —PAULO FREIRE, *PEDAGOGY OF THE OPPRESSED*[1]

STRATEGIES FOR DISMANTLING THE WALLS OF PHARAOH'S HOUSE

According to the biblical account, Moses never made it to the Promised Land (Deut 34:1–6). Moses was allowed to see the future home of his people from the hills above the Jordan River, but it would fall

---

1. Paulo Freire, *Pedagogy of the Oppressed*, trans. Myra Bergman Ramos (New York: Continuum, 1970), 42.

to his successor, Joshua, to lead the people into the territory their God had promised to their ancestors. Moses' conversion and faith journey enabled him to enter into the wider journey of the Hebrew people but not to see its completion.

Moses' faith required that he put his trust in God and believe his efforts would be used for God's ends. Faith also required that Moses relinquish the need to see the completion of the journey or the success of his life's work. By putting himself in solidarity with the oppressed people of Egypt, he was freed from the confines of pharaoh's house, but he also had to give up the security, stability, and identity his place in Egyptian society afforded. His solidarity with the people of Israel sent him wandering in the desert for the rest of his life, uncertain ultimately of his own success or the results of his efforts. Nevertheless, the book of Deuteronomy reports that, at the end of his life, overlooking the home he would never enter, Moses sang a song of thanksgiving for the blessings he and his people had received (Deut 31:30–32:44). Ultimately, the good life that Moses achieved was not measured in terms of material success, social stability, or personal achievement, but in faithfulness to his relationship with God and the plan God had for the people of Israel.

Personal conversion allows one to break free of the fundamental contradictions that confront every person, but it does not insure that any person's journey will find a final and simple resolution in this life. To lead a good life does not necessarily imply or require that a person lead a perfect life or that chance and death will not limit and even diminish the most heroic human efforts. For Christians, the good life is rooted in the faithfulness of the individual to God and the willingness of a person to trust in God even in the face of sorrow, failure, and death. Openness to holistic conversion and solidarity with the poor are the genuine marks of Christian faith. Success or failure in the practical affairs of this world are often disconnected and even in contradiction to the characteristics of faith.

If the option for the poor authenticates personal conversion, then the purpose of a theology of conversion is to create the conditions of genuine empathy and literal collaboration with the poor of the world as Gustavo Gutiérrez indicated. The primary, and indeed almost definitive, goal of a spirituality of liberation in a North American context will be to establish solidarity with the poor and oppressed.

This solidarity is essential because in many ways the destiny of the converted lies in the hands of the poor. Those who occupy the place of the oppressors in any historical world order must strive to break down the barriers that walled them into their own self-sufficiency and inertia. The first step in liberation of the oppressors is to disrupt the normal social and cultural ethos that disables them from knowing that they even need to be liberated. Dismantling the walls that keep many North Americans safe and secure in a prison of false values and inauthentic existence connotes the basic and fundamental priority of Christians concerned with authentic conversion.

This chapter will explore three ways Christians can respond to the structural and social dimensions of entrapment that many Americans experience. First, the chapter will articulate how one might cultivate authentic individual autonomy, which involves developing an understanding of the individual as inherently social and communal. Second, the chapter will return to the notion of mimetic desire, understood now not in terms of the values of a free-market society but rather as directing the natural human desire and tendency to imitate others toward the Christian tradition of imitating Christ. Third, it will discuss the development of hopefulness, as opposed to superficial optimism. Cultivating individual autonomy through social relationships, cultivating success through imitation of Christ, and developing hopefulness through acquiring a new understanding of what the future holds—three strategies for dismantling the walls of pharaoh's house—help people live according to the values of justice, mercy, generosity, and forgiveness. The goal of life in this sense is to form and actively share in a community that works toward the common good of all and thereby accomplishes the Christian understanding of God's will.

CULTIVATING GENUINE AUTONOMY THROUGH PARTICIPATION IN COMMUNITY

This book has argued that radical individualism and its corollary, a type of palliative culture, so pervade the American popular ethos that Christianity often casts itself in terms of this ideology. A genuinely Christian spirituality in this cultural milieu needs to recast the language of the spiritual journey so that individual Christians can discover their unique individuality and personal relationship with God in a social and communal context. This approach should also challenge Christian individuals and communities to see the fullness of their spiritual journey in radical forms of self-offering and sharing, especially with the poor and oppressed of this world. Certain strains of American thought have attempted to articulate precisely this approach to individuality and to develop a language that adequately reflects the human need for personal autonomy and fulfillment.

Perhaps ahead of his time, Josiah Royce (1855–1916), in his "Philosophy of Loyalty"[2] and *The Problem of Christianity*,[3] set out to challenge the very assumptions and attitudes that now ground the palliative culture. Royce wanted to provide a morally coherent alternative to the purely individualistic worldview that he observed developing, yet an alternative that would take the legitimate and positive insights of human growth and fulfillment seriously. What Royce found most troubling about the cultural mentality is "the divine right to be selfish" that is its cornerstone, and he saw the deification of utilitarian and expressive individualism, pragmatism, and their palliative implications as not only morally suspect and practically unworkable but also as ultimately self-defeating.[4] He wanted to show that a quest for personal self-fulfillment and autonomy does not have to lead to myopic and self-centered individualism.

Royce did not reject individualism, but he envisioned individuality to develop as Dorothy's did in *The Wizard of Oz*, not as Kevin's did in *Home Alone*, as discussed in chapter 3. In other words, Royce maintained that individualism emerged out of a communal process comprised of mutual sharing of gifts and talents rather than simply being revealed by the raw experience of defining oneself "against" the rest of society. Royce grounded his entire system on the belief that ultimate moral authority resides in the individual. Furthermore, he asserted that for a system to be ethical, it must ensure the attainment

---

2. Josiah Royce, "The Philosophy of Loyalty," in *The Basic Writings of Josiah Royce*, ed. with introduction by John J. McDermott (Chicago: University of Chicago Press, 1969), 2:855–1013.

3. Josiah Royce, *The Problem of Christianity*, with an introduction by John E. Smith (Chicago: University of Chicago Press, 1968).

4. Ibid., 881.

of an individual's highest good. An impersonal moral code, in Royce's view, cannot override personal autonomy and fulfillment. However, Royce would also insist that neither self-knowledge nor autonomy is possible without a fundamental personal commitment to some cause or purpose greater than oneself. Royce calls this fundamental commitment "loyalty."

For many people, *loyalty* is one of those words that connotes an antiquated, naive, and even dangerous attitude of blind faith and unreflective obedience to external authority or hollow moral codes. Loyalty does not represent a virtue that many modern-day Americans would think worthy of cultivation. However, Royce used *loyalty* in a much richer and more meaningful way, challenging humans to move beyond their preconceived notions to envision a virtue capable of standing against the dominant ethos.

Royce defined *loyalty* as "the willing and practical thoroughgoing devotion of a person to a cause . . . in a sustained and practical way."[5] Such loyalty calls people to make decisions and shape their lives in terms of the chosen cause, directing their activities, defining their other commitments, and limiting their personal responses to other feelings, desires, and impulses. *Fidelity, devotion,* and *solidarity* are other terms that come to mind. As understood by Royce, loyalty would seem to be wholly antithetical to the popular notion of individualism.

Royce would argue, however, that far from betraying a person's obligation to seek his or her highest good, loyalty is the only means possible to achieve this end. As Royce stated, "Be an individual; seek your own individual good; seek that good thoroughly, unswervingly, unsparingly, with all your heart and soul. However, I persist in asking: Where, in heaven above and in earth beneath, have you to look for your highest good? Where can you find it?"[6]

Without loyalty, people can never discover the highest good they seek or clarify and express their own deepest personal aspirations and possibilities: a person cannot come to know himself or herself in a void. The inner life is a tangle of emotions, needs, and desires that can find no unity within itself. Furthermore, the self is not wholly

---

5. Ibid., 861; Royce, *Problem*, 132.

6. Royce, "The Philosophy of Loyalty," 886.

preexistent but develops over time in a kind of dialogue with the outer world. Social training shapes one's desires and forms one's will; the inner self responds to this social training and tries to make sense out of it. So there is an ongoing interplay between social stimuli and internal appropriation and internal stimuli and external development and expression. Without some sort of overriding direction, however, this process can become circular, the activities and decisions stemming from it often arbitrary and contradictory. As advocated by a palliative culture, the process of sorting out one's feelings through introspection and communication is ultimately self-defeating if there is no goal or referent. So what can possibly give order and direction to this process?

Royce argued that active self-possession is the highest good for which the self can strive. Moreover, he asserted, people take possession of their lives by freely choosing some cause to be faithful to, because only fidelity to a cause gives order, coherence, and continuity to human identity. Only an individual with a coherent sense of identity can make any sort of informed and autonomous decisions; claims to independence are empty if there is no identifiable self to be called free. In Royce's words, announcing independence without commitment is the same as "proclaiming moral sovereignty over your life, without any definite life over which to be sovereign."[7] Precisely through denying oneself, giving oneself to others, and sacrificing oneself does one come into fullest possession of a self to be denied, given, and sacrificed. Without embracing an external cause, the individual remains hopelessly bound to the vicissitudes of sheer contingency and the demands of arbitrary and conflicting desires.

Critical to Royce's philosophy is his understanding of conscience, that mental capacity that allows one to pass judgment, correct or mistaken, on moral questions when they arise. As such, it is the faculty in which a person's most basic self-identity resides. Royce did not consider this capacity innate but viewed it as the interiorization of some plan of life, some idealized self that becomes the grounding for all decisions and choices. Further, by unifying the life of the individual, this plan constitutes the personality; it is what gives purpose and identity to the matrix of elements called the self. Royce

---

7. Ibid., 891.

defines a person as a "human life lived according to a plan,"[8] and the conscience helps an individual follow that ideal, on an ongoing basis. Because the purpose is ultimately beyond immediate fulfillment, the conscience facilitates recommitment to the cause, moment by moment. This is what Royce calls loyalty.

Only loyalty can unify the self. Only loyalty can lead to the development of conscience. Only loyalty can bring about self-possession and authentic humanity, in Royce's view. Without loyalty, there is only an inarticulate striving to be an individual entity. Without loyalty, Royce maintained, life is simply a "cauldron of seething and bubbling efforts to be somebody, a cauldron which boils dry when life ends."[9] This type of loyalty is profoundly expressed in this meditation on love by Pedro Arrupe, a Christian spiritual leader of the twentieth century:

> Nothing is more practical than finding God, that is, falling
>   in love in a quite absolute, final way.
> What you are in love with, what seizes your imagination,
>   will effect everything.
> It will decide what will get you out of bed in the morning,
>   what you will do with your evenings, how you will spend
>   your weekends,
>   what you read, who you know, what breaks your heart, and
>   what amazes you with joy and gratitude.
> Fall in love, stay in love, and it will decide everything.[10]

For Royce, the main issue is not whether a person should be freely and totally devoted to a cause; that is a fundamental requirement. Rather, the main questions are these: To what cause should one be loyal? Where, practically speaking, does one find and live out this cause?

In answer to the first question, Royce acknowledged that there are dubious and even evil causes to which people can, and often do,

---

8. Ibid., 921.

9. Ibid., 922–23.

10. Pedro Arrupe, "Rooted and Grounded in Love," in *One Jesuit's Spiritual Journey: Autobiographical Conversations of Pedro Arrupe with Jean-Claude Dietsch, S.J.* (St. Louis: Institute of Jesuit Sources, 1982/1986), 105–60.

devote themselves. While Royce believed that loyalty to even to a bad cause was better than a wholly dissolute life, he also formulated a standard by which to judge the value of a cause. As Royce stated, "In choosing and in serving the cause to which you are to be loyal, be, in any case, loyal to loyalty."[11] In other words, choose causes that may bring more loyalty, fidelity, and commitment to the world, not less. I believe that what Royce meant about being "loyal to loyalty" is quite similar to what Pope John Paul II means by the term *solidarity*. Solidarity is not merely a "feeling of vague compassion or shallow distress at the misfortunes of so many people, both near and far. On the contrary, it is a firm and persevering determination to commit oneself to the common good. That is to say to the good of all and of each individual, because we all are really responsible for all."[12] For John Paul II, solidarity presumed an underlying "interdependence" of relationship between people at every social level, an interdependence that transforms individuals and communities into an "ever more committed unity."[13]

Pope John Paul II also indicated that Christians have an obligation to analyze and challenge the causes to which other people are committed, especially if these causes distort or oppose the common good. The goal should be to help people find a more worthy focus for their loyal sentiments.

Solidarity does not necessarily require some remote or abstract, all-encompassing cause that transcends all day-to-day concerns. On the contrary, solidarity is most often needed among the commonplace: honesty in business, courtesy in public, civic responsibility, devotion to family, and religious vocation are all examples of

---

11. Royce, "The Problem of Loyalty," 929.

12. John Paul II, Encyclical Letter, *Sollicitudo rei socialis*, 38: AAS 80 (1988), 565–66. This is a major theme of his pontificate. Extensive discussions on this topic are found particularly in the above-mentioned encyclical and in the encyclical *Laborem exercens* (1981) and *Centesimus annus* (1991). John Paul II elucidates how this principle is central to the whole history of Catholic social teaching by stating, "What we nowadays call the principle of solidarity . . . is frequently stated by Pope Leo XIII, who uses the term 'friendship.' . . . Pope Pius XI refers to it with the equally meaningful term 'social charity.' Pope Paul VI expanding the concept to cover many modern aspects of the social question speaks of 'civilization of love.'" (*Centisimus annus*, 10: AAS 83 (1991), 805.

13. See by the Catholic Church, *Compendium of the Social Doctrine of the Church* (Washington, DC: USCCB Publishing, 2005), 192.

solidarity. These causes can be universalized: one can be devoted not just to one's family, for instance, but also to the cause of protecting family life in general. If one is willing to include in even the most mundane commitment an openness and concern for the general cause of solidarity, that particular loyalty can be of universal value and can lead to a general increase in the goodness of the world.

The Hope of the Beloved Community

Royce maintained that there is no great science to choosing one's particular cause; most people choose causes that are presented to them largely by chance and circumstance. However, the individual is fundamentally free in selecting which particular cause might become the defining focus of his or her life.[14] This cause should be true to the nature of the person; it should build on the natural talents, predispositions, and resources that one already has; it should unify and direct life, not completely recreate it.[15] Clearly, all people in the course of their lives will be presented with a number of valid possibilities. For example, a chance visit to the zoo might awaken an interest in animal welfare that could open into a lifetime of involvement with animal shelters or conservation societies. Or witnessing an interaction between a police officer and a homeless person might create an interest in legal assistance leading to a career as a public defender. To address the second main question, how does a person choose one good cause over another or stick with a good cause if a seemingly better one presents itself? No one can know the outcome of a choice when it is made, but it is not the cause itself that is especially important; the loyalty to it and solidarity with it are what are essential.

In Royce's view, self-sacrifice or even suffering is not a valid reason for breaking a commitment. Suffering is endemic to the human condition, but suffering for the sake of a cause gives meaning not only to the cause but also to the suffering. Fidelity is not simply a virtue, it is a fundamental necessity for any meaningful existence, and true freedom is grounded in loyalty to a commitment. In other

---

14. Royce, "The Philosophy of Loyalty," 898–903.

15. Ibid., 905–10.

words, freedom, autonomy, and self-possession are inseparable from active and decisive fidelity to some worthy cause greater than oneself. Loyalty is profoundly social. The concept of loyalty clearly implies that no person can be fully human outside of a social context or apart from social bonds. A commitment draws us into a community of other people who have embraced the same cause that we have, so a commitment to the cause is inherently a commitment to the other people loyal to the same cause. And the interpersonal bonding that results reinforces the strength of our loyalty. This is why the term *solidarity* resonates so strongly with Royce's understanding of true individuality.

Devoted to superhuman causes, people in solidarity with one another are united at a deeper level than that of mutual consent. Furthermore, true solidarity implies a direct involvement in the social institutions that give society concrete shape. Solidarity creates bridging communities that Harvard sociologist Robert Putnam finds to be an essential component of civic order. For example, to be a devoted member of a religious community implies a commitment to religion in general, not just to a specific group of people. Institutions and commitments are never impersonal, but they are always greater than the personal element. All loyalty is based in a unity that transcends the concrete manifestation of that unity and, therefore, cannot be exhausted.

Royce proposed a philosophical explanation for this fundamental relationship between the individual and community.[16] Basically, society is a person-shaping process, forming individuals by guiding them into a communal existence of unity and purpose. In turn, each community functions as a single unit, bonding a group of individuals into a single mind acting together as one in time and in a larger social context. This community is itself only fully a community when it enters into a wider community of communities and takes on a specific role and purpose analogous to that of an individual within a community. For example, one might lobby legislators for a particular human-rights law, but in the process, the individual

---

16. Royce, *The Problem of Christianity*, 194–95. For a more thorough account of Royce's analysis of this point, see John Markey, "Clarifying the Relationship between the Universal and Particular Churches through the Philosophy of Josiah Royce," *Philosophy & Theology* 15:2 (2003): 299–320.

could be drawn into a community of like-minded neighbors acting with a common purpose. In turn, the neighborhood community could find common cause with other groups throughout the county or state and join with them in a common goal greater than any that a single individual could have envisioned. According to Royce, people can be fully human and uniquely individual only if they live in ways that promote social bonds constituting real communities that in turn form wider communities of love and service to the greater good of humanity.[17]

Royce maintained that God's beloved community is the ideal universalizing vision of solidarity. In the *Problem of Christianity* he stated,

> The Kingdom of Heaven is a perfectly lived unity of individual men joined in one divine chorus—a unity of men who, except through their attachment to this life which exists on the level of the beloved community of the Kingdom of Heaven, would be breeders of woe, would be lost souls. . . . For the ethical side of the doctrine of life is not what you find, but what you create.[18]

REDIRECTING MIMETIC DESIRE: FROM ENVY TO CHRIST

Chapter 3 discussed René Girard's notion of mimetic desire and the way in which it shapes the human need to imitate others in order to know anything. One dimension of this type of desire correlates with the ancient Judeo-Christian vice of envy or covetousness. That chapter also analyzed aspects of North American culture, attempting to demonstrate how the ideology of free-market capitalism distorts the phenomena of envy often portraying it as a necessary catalyst for economic activity and thereby elevating it from a vice to a type of virtue. In order to dismantle the walls that imprison many North Americans, it is necessary to offer an alternative to the ideology of

---

17. For Royce, this reality is precisely what is meant be the traditional moral term *conscience*. Ibid, 913–33.

18. Royce, *The Problem of Christianity*, 196.

free-market capitalism and to the form of mimetic desire understood primarily as envy.

Logical Alternatives to a Free-market Society

As previously discussed, Karl Polanyi challenges the foundational assumptions on which free-market capitalism rests. He debunks the liberal creed and forcefully demonstrates that the whole notion of self-regulating free markets is a utopian theory that cannot be sustained over time.[19] By characterizing the system as *utopian*, Polanyi means that free-market capitalism is an economic hypothesis that cannot be proven and that history reveals to be untrue.[20] An entire belief system—and the Liberal Creed is a belief system—was constructed around the false idol of the free market. Polanyi rightfully shows that the irrational faith in the efficiency, necessity, and value of self-regulating free markets is dangerous and unsustainable.[21] He argues that contemporary society must discard this false belief system that elevates economic life over every other dimension of social life and instead acknowledge that economic life is inherently embedded in a whole web of human social relationships.[22]

According to Polanyi, the expansion of the free-market economy into the free-market society indicates a fundamental failure of both logic and morality within the societies that allowed this to happen.[23] While markets may deliver goods and services to the most number of people in the most efficient way, he insisted that certain aspects of human life cannot be objectified and sold as commodities.[24] At the most basic level, land, labor, and money are not commodities but forms of human relationship; they mediate essential sources of human life and identity. Furthermore, the distribution of necessities such as health care, education, housing, food, and clothing cannot be handled adequately by or left to market forces; they are also not

---

19. Polanyi, *The Great Transformation*, 71–80.

20. Ibid., 3.

21. Ibid., 141–57.

22. Ibid., 171–86

23. Ibid., 267.

24. Ibid., 71–80.

commodities that a self-adjusting free market should be allowed to dictate and control.

Polanyi called on societies to reclaim their social interpretation of human life and put economics in their proper perspective: at the service of human social relations and the fulfillment of human needs.[25] A free-market system is neither the source nor the salvation of any society. The long-term well-being of any community lies in its ability to treat human relationships with respect, to properly understand the vital role that human dignity and self-worth play in social and cultural organization and advancement, and to fully appreciate the inherent interrelationship of humans and their ecological context.

Interpreting human social life in this way leads to a fundamentally different hypothesis about economics. For Polanyi, this hypothesis is not the dialectic opposite of the free market—communism or fascism[26]—but a type of political and economic system that has free markets and participates in wider international markets but with serious levels of government oversight and regulation to ensure that the market does not take priority over the good of the society. A society such as Polanyi envisions will realize that the fair distribution of wealth, particularly that which derives from land and land use, is necessary so that all in the society have some share in its prosperity and sacrifice judiciously in its need. This does not mean that there will not be inequalities of income and wealth in the society but simply that all have some opportunity to share in the general wealth of the society.

To achieve this end, a democratic government must adequately regulate markets, must institute taxation based on the realization that some redistribution of wealth will always need to occur, and must not use or allow businesses to use money to unfairly create wealth and manipulate the value of goods. Money itself should function to mediate human relationships by facilitating the exchange of goods and services to the benefit of all. Money must represent real markets and not fictitious ones existing solely to generate profits for investors while skewing the overall level of value for real objects in the marketplace.

---

25. Ibid., 257–67.
26. Ibid., 242–56.

By exposing the fiction of the self-regulating free-market utopia, Polanyi also uncovers the false understanding of the human
that grounds this utopian vision.[27] Humans should not be primarily
understood as a species whose activities and habits are solely dic-
tated by economic factors and mimetic desires. An interpretation
of human life that considers base human desires such as envy, pride,
greed, and unlimited ambition as natural and therefore good needs to
be discredited as well. By creating distrust and resentment at the core
of human communities, these human desires disrupt social life at its
core; they cloud right reason and clear judgment with acrimony and
animosity. When a society nurtures these feelings, it cannot move
toward a more genuine human community that promotes social fair-
ness and the common good. Without denying the fundamental need
for humans to imitate and strive for excellence, the Judeo-Christian
tradition offers an alternative account of the proper ends for these
natural tendencies. This tradition enables the very kind of shared,
trusting, and gracious interrelationships that Polanyi finds necessary
to sustain a truly human existence.

Imago Dei: Imitating Christ Imitating God

The tradition of Christian anthropology is grounded on the presup-
position that humans are made in the image and likeness of God
(Gen 1:26–27). The belief that humans are made in the image of
their creator implies that they have the unique desire and ability
to know their creator and share in the attributes of this divine life.
Christians believe that in Jesus Christ, God the creator is revealed to
be triune in nature: a communion of three divine persons—Father,
Son, and Spirit—who mutually and fully participate with each other
in such a way that they have a single shared life. This understanding
of human existence—that they are created in the image of the triune God—implies that they too are inherently created social beings
that participate and share in the lives of one another and God. To be
fully human then in this tradition means to live in the highest form
of communion of life with God and one's neighbors. Furthermore,
Christians insist that this communion of life does not diminish one's

---

27. Ibid., 257–67.

individuality but rather brings it to its highest level of development by giving it a context and purpose that transcends mere selfishness. In the thought of Saint Paul, a "mere individual" does not fully exist at all but is in fact cut off from the most basic sources of life and vitality (1 Cor 12:12–31).[28] Jesus similarly invites his disciples to imitate him as he imitates God by sharing his own life in the effort to help people deepen their inherent relationship with God and one another (Jn 13:33–35, 14:11–14). For Christians this fullness of life can only be achieved through a kind of self-offering and gift of self to a higher purpose and greater communion of persons (Jn 14–17).

In Christian anthropology, the good life is both joyful and moral simultaneously. In a life in which there is genuine sharing of one's gifts and possibilities and in which one both gives to others and graciously receives in return, a greater good is achieved for all. When human life has a transcendent purpose, mimetic desire is not extinguished but replaced with a drive to desire what God desires, to see what God sees, to act like God acts (see especially the Sermon on the Mount in Matthew 5, and particularly verses 43–48). When one interprets life from God's point of view, envy is transformed into magnanimity and pride is replaced by the desire to outdo the other in giving freely, showing mercy and loving unconditionally.

In the New Testament tradition exemplified by Saint Paul, the fullness of life comes when one is worthy of imitation by others: "imitate me as I imitate Christ" (1 Cor 4:16–17, 11:1). This cycle of imitation of God replaces the spiral of animosity and violence caused by envy and pride as the most complete description of human life. Christian anthropology fulfills Polanyi's vision of the rediscovery of the fundamental necessity of community and a social interpretation of individual life to put economics in its proper perspective. Economic activity, in Christian anthropology, no longer serves as the battlefield where the competition for the acquisition of more and more goods is acted out but rather the market in the center of the social life where goods and services are distributed in a way that no one goes hungry or lives in need (Acts 2:42–47, 4:32–36). An authentic communion of life insures that there is a fundamental

---

28. For the most extensive and thoughtful analysis of the communal nature of Pauline thought, see Jerome Murphy-O'Connor, *Becoming Human Together: The Pastoral Anthropology of St. Paul* (Wilmington, DE: Michael Glazier Press, 1982).

understanding that all members of the society have gifts to share and that the sharing of all gifts by all members not only creates a good society but also good persons whose potential can be fully realized.

This Christian anthropology can also represent a utopia that is both pre-rational and irrational. This utopia is pre-rational in that it is fundamentally based on the universal intuition of humans that there is some higher life, higher power, and higher purpose that they are called upon to acknowledge and pursue. It is only irrational however, if it is not logically interpreted in the form of real human judgments and actions that enable it to exist in the present. In other words, if the utopia is only a vision of a future life that its adherents dismiss as unachievable and, therefore, not morally binding, then it functions irrationally as an ideology that will be used to advance or deter other types of human behavior but will have no positive embodiment. Jesus taught his disciples to begin living the future—what he called the Reign of God—immediately in the present. Jesus insisted that imitating God was not a utopian dream but a practical moral claim on the day-to-day lives of those who embraced it (Mt 5:43–48). While the ultimate fulfillment of the Reign of God may lie in the historical future, it exists presently whenever God's Spirit is acting to bring about the literal shared life it requires. For Christians, the logic of the Reign of God is precisely that it is not utopia but a revelation from God of the real way that humans exist and should behave.

Christian anthropology does not necessarily dismiss or diminish the pervasiveness of original sin in human life and history. In the Catholic tradition, the natural world is not utterly depraved or deprived of the capability of some good action and unable to contribute positively to its own history and redemption. In Catholic thought, God chooses to make humans co-creators of the world in the sense that through their lives and actions they can participate in God's saving plan for all creation. Here salvation is mysterious but not mystical—God mysteriously engages humans and history in order to create an eternal pattern whereby chance is coaxed from utter randomness to a certain aesthetic alignment by the necessity of love, and the Creator lures order from chaos in a systematic yet complex way. God works with creation to gently urge and nurture it so that what is false will yield to what is true, the wrong to the right, the ugly to the beautiful, evil to the good, and the polluted to the holy.[29] Providence acts with humans to re-create a world in which a genuine communion between persons and with the divine life becomes not only possible but also the inevitable destiny of history.

In Catholic theology God's mysterious Providence is rooted not just in human cooperation and interpersonal sharing but also ultimately in the power God has to bring justice and peace out of suffering, evil, and sinful acts. This never implies that suffering, evil, and sin are good or somehow not fully negative and destructive. Evil is power that always works to negate God's plan for the world. Evil acts and human suffering remain historical facts that God does not erase or minimize. Nevertheless, the Christian tradition gives witness that God has the power to atone for these historical realities and uses history itself and human willingness to share in God's efforts to transform the effects of these sorrowful deeds toward ends that God desires. The power of atonement is God's response to evil and sin, and it is a power that God extends to us as a necessary component of creating a good life and communion of life.

The concept of atonement used here does not refer to the substitution theory of atonement often attributed to the medieval Christian theologian Anselm and brought to its fullest articulation in the thought of the Protestant Christian theologian John Calvin.[30] Calvin proposes that Jesus atones for human sin by taking the full brunt of God's rage and anger at our human disobedience on himself thereby saving humans from the punishment that should be theirs. From the Catholic perspective, this is not the logical inference from the broad witness of scripture that consistently describes a God who not only loves humanity and shares the divine life with it but also continually works to restore broken relationships with it through extravagant acts of love and mercy. In the Catholic view, through both the creation and redemption of the world and human history, God demonstrates truly unconditional and self-sacrificing love. It is this type of love

---

29. For this insight I am indebted Greg Zuschlag's reflections to me on the metaphysics of C. S. Peirce.

30. For a particularly thoughtful and sympathetic explanation of the substitution theory of atonement and some contemporary alternatives, see Leanne Van Dyk, "How Does Jesus Make a Difference?" in *Essentials of Christian Theology*, ed. William C. Placher (Louisville, KY: Westminster John Knox Press, 2003), 205–18.

that is atoning of human sin and tragedy and that finally replaces the logic of the marketplace with the logic of atoning love.

Atonement in this sense appears as a needed response to envy throughout scripture.[31] Joseph atoned for the envy of his brothers not by "paying them back" when the time came, but by extending a new relationship of generosity and communion out of his prosperity (Gen 37–46). Similarly, God does not use the crucifixion of Jesus to exact revenge against those whose envy and pride blinded them to Jesus' message of love and forgiveness. Rather, God used this despicable act as a means of changing the whole dynamic of history to the good by raising Jesus from the dead and continuing his life and ministry in a universal and historically everlasting way through the creation of the church and the gift of his own Spirit to the whole world. This radical form of self-giving goes beyond mere sharing or even forgiveness, and actually creates the conditions for some new historical opportunity to re-create the broken bonds of community and the shredded social fabric caused by evil acts.

In this sense, atonement is an action on the part of the victim to restore the web of intricate personal relationships upon which a community depends that have been damaged, sometimes deeply, by sinful actions on the part of some or all of the members of the community. Atonement implies a kind of self-sacrificing and self-offering love that comes not out of one's weakness (as in the case of codependent behavior) but out of the mysterious power of that love to create something new. Atoning love assumes that humans are empowered by love to give of themselves in ways that create and sustain life even after the devastating effects of sin and sorrow. The logic of atoning love is the antidote to the tragedy of American life that creates a boundless desire for that which cannot be attained and a need that can never be fulfilled by even the acquisition of what was sought.

Christians believe that when humans imitate God through acts of atoning love and radical sharing, the tragic tide of history literally changes. The power of God's providence to urge history to its final destiny cooperates with human freedom to historically embody the vision that God has for creation. By readily sharing their gifts with others and desiring to be like Christ and God, people can overcome

---

31. See further Royce, *The Problem of Christianity*, 202–8.

the power of envy and pride and reorient their natural human desire to a divine purpose. Natural human desires operating with God's supernatural presence and power connote a logically different alternative to that of free-market capitalism. One leads to a new and hopeful future for humanity and the other only to an endless and winless war of "all against all." The latter is ultimately a vision of chaos and despair for those who embrace it and this fact is not without dire consequences for societies who accept it uncritically and irrationally as common sense.

DEVELOPING AN AESTHETIC OF HOPE

Accomplishing the long-term and complex task of dismantling the walls of pharaoh's house will depend on sociopolitical conversion among a broad and diverse spectrum of the North American population. Critical to the emergence of authentic sociopolitical conversion is genuine hope that people can work together to realize a future, fundamentally different than present reality (as discussed in chapter 5). The task remains for Christians and other religiously converted persons to fully articulate a vision of a hopeful future—a vision that moves beyond the superficial optimism (see chapter 4) that often characterizes the American ethos.

Reimagining the Beautiful

What would a hopeful aesthetic look like? What is an example of a hopeful artistic expression in American life? Writing at the turn of the twentieth century, W.E.B. DuBois asked these same questions. In his famous book on racial inequality in America, *The Souls of Black Folks*, DuBois asserts that the artistic expression arising from the experience of slavery actually comprises the most original and significant understanding of the beautiful in American history.[32] Analyzing the development and composition of the "Negro Spiritual," DuBois finds this musical tradition not only artistically compelling but also surprisingly hopeful:

---

32. W.E.B. DuBois, *The Souls of Black Folk* (New York: Bantam Classic Edition, 1989), 177–88.

Little of beauty has America given the world save the rude grandeur God himself stamped on her bosom; the human spirit in this new world has expressed itself in vigor and ingenuity rather than in beauty. And so by fateful chance the Negro folk-song—the rhythmic cry of the slave—stands to-day not simply as the sole American music, but as the most beautiful expression of human experience born this side the seas. It has been neglected, it has been, and is, half despised, and above all it has been persistently mistaken and misunderstood; but notwithstanding, it still remains as the singular spiritual heritage of the nation and the greatest gift of the Negro people.[33]

Though the twentieth century would engender a whole new era in American artistic expression, DuBois asserts that spiritual songs are born out of the experience of slavery.[34] This makes them all the more remarkable in that what they offer most of all is an incredible hope in the power of God even in the midst of the most dehumanizing kind of imprisonment. DuBois notes some examples of songs, including the following three, which express hope in the face of sorrow and evil:

I walk through the churchyard
To lay this body down;
I know moon-rise, I know star-rise;
I walk in the moonlight, I walk in the starlight;
I'll lie in the grave and stretch out my arms,
I'll go to judgment in the evening of the day,
And my soul and thy soul shall meet that day,
When I lay this body down.

✧ ✧ ✧

Oh, the stars in the elements are falling,
And the moon drips away into blood,

---

33. Ibid., 178.
34. Ibid.

And the ransomed of the Lord are returning unto God,
Blessed be the name of the Lord.

❖ ❖ ❖

Michael, haul the boat ashore,
Then you'll hear the horn they blow,
Then you'll hear the trumpet sound,
Trumpet sound the world around,
Trumpet sound for rich and poor,
Trumpet sound the Jubilee,
Trumpet sound for you and me.[35]

Far from the nihilistic despair or the "howl" of most mid-twentieth-century American art, the songs of the enslaved demonstrate a moral fortitude and a solemn peacefulness in the face of an impossible situation, and the singers look forward to the day of judgment and the possibilities of renewal that await them after death. In song after song, African American slaves and segregated populations affirm their trust in God's infinite care for them and the justice that God will bring.

Martin Luther King Jr. relied on these spirituals to invigorate the language of the American civil rights movement in the 1950s and 1960s.[36] What he termed his "radiant hope," namely that God could "weave a tapestry of redemption" out of the tangled web of human wickedness, found its roots in the simple rhythms and words of slavery's songs. These songs and words do not seek consolation in wishful thinking, in some vague dream of life in heaven after death, or in the simplistic desire that one's soul will find happiness in some future ethereal existence. The words used in spirituals and in the civil rights movement give concrete expression to the most basic tenets of the Christian faith: the resurrection of the body, the second coming of Jesus Christ to judge the living and the dead, and the transformation of the sorrows of this life into the "new and everlasting Jerusalem" through the atoning love of God.

---

35. Ibid., 185–86.

36. Martin Luther King Jr., *The Strength to Love* (New York: Harper and Row, 1960), 100.

When truly believed, these Christian doctrines exhort Christians to engage in heroically transformative action in this life under the steadfast assurance that they are doing the only thing that truly lasts. Even in the darkest hours of slavery, segregation, and invisibility, African Americans held on to an unquenchable vision of the beautiful designs of the Almighty and their participation in it. This aesthetic vision had the power to unite communities under the direst of circumstances and to embolden action for change in the midst of unfathomable hostility.

Time has passed. For some, the hopeful fire of the civil rights movement has dimmed or is even unknown. Some social critics worry that American society has embraced shallow, feel-good forms of language and art that support a cheerful but ultimately superficial optimism.[37] At the beginning of the twenty-first century, can American culture relearn the message of hope that carried the oppressed through such terrible tribulations? Can Americans embrace the radiant hope to which their own inequities once gave birth?

Christian Hope

The heaven popularly imagined in American culture is a lot like a family reunion in which there will be a lot of hugging, even possibly by God.[38] Most Americans, including those who believe in an afterlife, have only vague ideas about the future beyond this life and its connection to personal identity, social relationships, and ethical decisions.[39] Often, rather than a clear expectation, the idea of heaven represents a wish or desire that there is something more after death and particularly that family and friends live on.[40] Even contemporary theology and Christian spiritualities tend to offer a minimalist view of heaven that is seldom clear and engaging.[41] The dearth of

---

37. Robert Bellah, et al., *The Good Society* (New York: Alfred A. Knopf, 1991), 19–51.

38. See further Colleen McDannell and Bernhard Lang, *Heaven: A History* (New Haven: Yale University Press, 1988), 307–13; they are referring particularly to an article by James Breig, "Beyond the Pearly Gates: What *US Catholic* Readers Believe about the Afterlife," *US Catholic* 48 (May 1983): 6–18.

39. Colleen McDaniel and Bernhard Lang, *Heaven: A History*, 307–52.

40. Ibid., 309–13.

41. Ibid., 335–49.

any realistic and compelling scenario of the next life similarly fails to illicit genuine hope that there exists a future that will be authentically redemptive of the injustices and tragedies of this life.[42]

According to the Christian theologian Donald Gelpi, hope forms the central catalyst propelling the converted to move beyond merely personal concerns to the kind of universal and transformative life necessary for full sociopolitical conversion. Gelpi describes the core relationship between hope and the Christian understanding of God:

> The perfection of human hopes by expanding them to include the universal, practical benevolence which the gospel inculcates and with which Jesus lived and died enables to attain a more humane, a more perfectly human, degree of perfection than we would if left to human nature's finite, distorted and sinful natural resource. . . . Only God, desires naturally and benevolently the good of everyone, even of sinners and of those adamantly opposed to God. The perfection of human hope, therefore, in teaching the human heart to hope with a divinely universal benevolence empowers sinful people to attain . . . a degree of human perfection which human nature could never attain left simply to itself.[43]

Genuine hope is a belief in some cause greater than the individual self that will have lasting and far-reaching benefit to a society and even the world as a whole.[44] For Christians, this cause is not merely a utopian ideal; neither is it ultimately rooted in any particular religious or political movement. For Christians, the ultimate source of all hope is in God (Rom 8:37–39).

In the Christian imagination, the future is in continuity with this life. Each person will have psychosomatic unity—that is, a physical embodiment—and the relationships that shaped and constituted each life will continue and grow. People from all parts of the world

---

42. Ibid., 345–52.

43. Donald Gelpi, *The Gracing of Human Experience*, 335.

44. For a further explanation of this understanding of the significance of hope for human social transformation, see Josiah Royce, *The Problem of Christianity*, 248–49.

and cultural traditions will converge into a single diverse communion of persons. All of creation will experience judgment and the righting of historical inequities and evils. In a single moment of transformation and renewal, this world will grow in love, freedom, and knowledge into a single glorious and joyous community. What's more, the Christian tradition articulates the view that this beautiful future is already present in history and human lives.

This theology derives from the New Testament, which is not so much a remembrance of the historical existence of an important teacher as it is a sustained reflection on the consequences for humanity of the life, death, and Resurrection of Jesus of Nazareth. Saint Paul in particular focuses not only on the memory of the Christian community but also on the radiant hope that Christ has revealed. This hope itself is not new, for it is completely rooted in the Hebrew scriptures' determined and unwavering belief in the power and justice of God. Throughout his letters and most explicitly in the Letter to the Romans, Paul articulates the consequences of this singular trust in the divine intentions for creation. Though only one of countless Christian formulations of this faith in God and the future that God ensures, Romans 8:19–39 is a classic example of this theme.

Each of the fives stanzas of this passage prominently declares complete confidence in God and God's vision for the fulfillment of God's plans. That God has a plan, one that is patient and slowly being realized even through adversity and human sinfulness, is central to this Christian interpretation of history. According to Paul, God patiently cooperates with human choices to weave a new creation out of the past. Paul sees all people "groaning" in anticipation (together with all creation) for our "adoption" into the family of God. While he describes those who believe in Christ as the "firstborn" in this future family, he implies that it will be wide and inclusive. Those who accept Christ now into their lives through baptism and allow Christ's Spirit to work within them are already being "conformed" into an image of Christ. They will have both a longing for and an anticipation of the fulfillment of God's promises.[45]

---

45. John Polkinghorne, *The God of Hope and the End of the World* (New Haven: Yale University Press, 2002), 88–89.

As Paul asserts and Christians believe, this is not a picture of some futuristic utopia but is a present reality, working through people and history to achieve its ultimate purposes. As Christians wait for the fullness of this rebirth to take place, they do so with full assurance through Jesus' bodily Resurrection of their own bodily redemption with its myriad relationships. In any present suffering, Christians find consolation in the belief that nothing in the universe can keep them from the love of God. Stretching from the deepest history of the Hebrew people to the present, God's promise to creation is fidelity and solidarity.

The Last Things

The hopefulness of the Christian vision is ultimately rooted in an interrelated set of doctrines about the end of time or the last things. According to Christian belief, the Resurrection of Jesus Christ from the dead entails the promise of a new future for humanity. The fullness of Christian hope rests in this promise.

In the centuries immediately after the life of Saint Paul and the earliest Christian communities, Christian thinkers developed a theology of "last things." This theology, debated and voted upon by the Christian leaders of the day, was first codified in the Nicene Creed at the first ecumenical council, held in Nicaea in 325, and is still part of the Christian Creed. The theology of last things consists of belief in the following: the resurrection of the body, the second coming of Jesus Christ to judge the living and the dead, the communion of saints, and life everlasting. Each of these contributes to a vision of genuine hope, as opposed to superficial optimism.

Resurrection of the Body

Not merely a representation of Jesus' execution, the cross stands as the organizing sign for the Christian interpretation of human life. It serves as the dynamic symbol of the Christian hope in the power of God to subvert evil, conquer death, and fulfill the promised future. In a rich and profound way, the cross signifies the whole Hebrew tradition of God's fidelity to God's covenant. It also gives concrete expression to Jesus' proclamation about God's beloved community and God's loving intentions for creation. While the crucifixion itself seems ugly, if not repellant, it becomes beautiful in its signification of the power of life to triumph over sin and death.[46] The dynamics of Christian hope transform the ugliness of a criminal execution into a symbol of the Divine's power to transform each human life. The cross enlivens in Christians not just hope for their personal survival but longing for a new form of earthly existence.

Most important to the Christian interpretation of resurrection is that it is a resurrection of the whole person, body and soul (known as psychosomatic unity). Unlike the Platonic and neo-Platonic Hellenistic interpretations of human existence, the Judeo-Christian tradition has consistently upheld the human as an integral relationship between a physical body and an animating spirit. After the pattern of Jesus' Resurrection, resurrection for Christians is likewise understood as an integral transformation of the whole person into a new form of existence.[47] The scriptural accounts of the empty tomb (Mt 28:5–6; Mk 16:6; Lk 24:4–5; Jn 20:1–9) vividly express the wholeness of Christian hopes for resurrection. The human body is not a simple adjunct to human life, and the next life is not an ethereal communion of souls detached from their physical bodies and the relationships and history that those bodies experienced. Rather, human bodies and everything they ever experience form each person into a distinct self that has a real and persistent identity. The resurrection verifies that the fullness of this identity perseveres into the future, when God will transform it into "the freedom of the glory of the children of God" (Rom 8:21).

---

46. See further Alejandro Garcia-Rivera, *The Community of the Beautiful: A Theological Aesthetics* (Collegeville, MN: Liturgical Press, 1999), 39–63, and *The Garden of God: A Theological Cosmology* (Minneapolis, MN: Fortress Press, 2009).

47. See Colleen McDannell and Bernhard Lang, *Heaven: A History*, for further discussion about the difference between anthropocentric and theocentric accounts of the future. McDannell and Lang argue that the theocentric view of heaven dominated the first two millennia of Christian thought. Rooted in a strong understanding of the nature and purpose of God, the theocentric view presumes that merely being in the presence of God is the highest destiny that humans can achieve and that contemplating this reality is itself the end of human longing and purpose. How humans are granted access to the divine presence dominates most discussions on the sin, grace, and the afterlife from this point of view. The anthropocentric view, which develops largely in the late nineteenth and early twentieth centuries, views heaven primarily as a stage of further human development and activity. Here the focus is largely on the saints and their happiness. As the authors' state, "In the anthropocentric heaven, where all attention was directed toward the saints—and not to God—motion, variety and endless diversity supplied the keys to eternal happiness" (304).

Resurrection, as Christians understand it, is not merely the resuscitation of a corpse, as Saint Paul makes quite clear: "Flesh and blood cannot inherit the kingdom of God, nor does the perishable inherit the imperishable. Listen, I will tell you a mystery! We will not all die, but we will all be changed, in a moment, in the twinkling of an eye, at the last trumpet. For the trumpet will sound, and the dead will be raised imperishable, and we will be changed. For this perishable body must put on imperishability, and this mortal body must put on immortality" (1 Cor 15:50–53). The Christian vision of resurrection asserts that the future will be continuous with the present but in a way that transforms and renews it dramatically. Human life is changed, not ended, in the teachings of Saint Paul.

While the New Testament never lays out the specific dynamics of this continuity and transformation of human existence, it does present some important clues as to what resurrection will look like. Although Paul's assertions are beautiful beyond comprehension, the resurrection of believers will not stop at simply continuing the limited historical forms of life that humans now experience. No one has the time or opportunity in this life to fulfill her or his individual destiny and potential. The next life must offer the possibility that God's "powerful but respectful divine grace"[48] will transform and purify people in ways that both respect their integrity and expand their opportunities to explore those dimensions of their lives that were left underdeveloped or untried in their historical lives. As Polkinghorne points out, "Ultimately, what was lost will be restored, and what of good that was never gained will be bestowed."[49] It is precisely this opportunity to realize the infinite potential of one's life that awakens the Christian imagination to the beauty of the cross.

The Second Coming of Jesus Christ to Judge the Living and the Dead

Often missing among Christians in the developed world is any real sense of the eschatological meaning of the second coming of Jesus and his role in a final judgment of humankind. To Christians living in pharaoh's house, Jesus' future reengagement in human

---

48. Polkinghorne, *The God of Hope*, 111.

49. Ibid.

history seems mythical at best. However, profound insights are often portrayed in mythic terms, most forms of language being inadequate to express the power of aesthetic vision. Although the risen Christ's future coming is an important dimension of many Christian subcultures, the dominant American ethos has often muted the idea of a second coming and the concept of divine judgment.

The wider Christian tradition however, has always strived to maintain the power of universal saving action of Christ manifest in his passion, death, and Resurrection. Likewise, most Christians hold the firm conviction that Jesus will come again to judge humanity according to the principles and virtues that he demonstrated during his own historical existence. Liberation theologians insist on this aspect of eschatology as absolutely central to the Christian vision of the end times,[50] maintaining that the poor and oppressed peoples of history are counting on Jesus Christ to return, bring about the justice he proclaimed, and right the wrongs of history as he promised. As recounted in the gospels, Jesus often talked about the actions that would lead people to union with God after death:

> "Come, you that are blessed by my Father, inherit the kingdom prepared for you from the foundation of the world; for I was hungry and you gave me food, I was thirsty and you gave me something to drink, I was a stranger and you welcomed me, I was naked and you gave me clothing, I was sick and you took care of me, I was in prison and you visited me." Then the righteous will answer him, "Lord, when was it that we saw you hungry and gave you food, or thirsty and gave you something to drink? And when was it that we saw you a stranger and welcomed you, or naked and gave you clothing? And when was it that we saw you sick or in prison and visited you?" And the king will answer them, "Truly I tell you, just as you did it to one of the least of these who are members of my family, you did it to me." (Mt 25:31–40)

According to the pattern of divine atonement that Jesus represents, the oppressed, despised, violated, and impoverished victims

---

50. See further Ignacia Ellacuria SJ and Jon Sobrino SJ, eds., *Mysterium Liberationis: Fundamental Concepts of Liberation Theology* (Maryknoll, NY: Orbis Books, 1993), 235–388.

of human history will have an opportunity to forgive and reconcile with their oppressors. Such a reconciliation makes no sense in human logic, but emboldened by the love of God and the power of God's animating Spirit, the "sinned-against" may choose to follow God's example and offer forgiveness and renewal to those who have wronged them. This is in no way a denial of sins committed, and no one is forced into forgiveness. In all of these ways, the final judgment will be a blessing—an offer of new life—to all who participate in it. The oppressed will receive their rightful place in creation and will achieve their full humanity. The oppressors will acknowledge the violence they inflicted on others and humbly accept divine judgment and divine forgiveness. By forgiving those who hurt them, the oppressed participate in divinity by communing in love with all of God's children, even those who do not deserve it. By admitting their guilt, the oppressors participate by acknowledging the equal standing of everyone, even those whose earthly lives had been miserable. While the process will be difficult and even painful, the creation of a new and just life gives humans hope in the future.

Communion of Saints

As discussed in chapter 3, Christians understand the divine plan as the creation of a community of communities in which each person receives his or her proper and unique place in a complex shared life of people from all times in history whom God has chosen to share God's divine life for eternity. In the Christian view, this communion of communions that Josiah Royce and Martin Luther King referred to as the Beloved Community is the ultimate future for all. The Christian faith asserts that this communion already exists: humans already participate in this communion if they desire to imitate Jesus and are filled with his Spirit. In this way Christians really are united, if invisibly, with all those who have loved God and done God's will throughout the ages. So the communion of saints is both a present experience of the faithful and the future hope of all humankind.

Life Everlasting

In the Hebrew world of Jesus and his predecessors, Hellenistic (Greek) interpretations of time had no meaning. Instead of portraying the Divine as existing outside of time, the Hebrew tradition portrayed God as connected to and participating in human history. While the Greek philosophers could not accept that a deity whose participation in human time would corrupt the divine essence in some way, Jesus and his forbears conceived of God as the creator of time and history and superior to them in every way. Although God always was and always will be, God does not exist outside of time. Thus, as Christians understand it, life in God may be everlasting, but it is not necessarily timeless. Christians believe that the human processes of growth and ongoing conversion require the passage of time, and that continued growth in love and virtue in the future is inherent in their hope of resurrection. Though they may have life in God, they expect to remain human. While the hoped for life to come will be a renovation and improvement of this life, it will not be wholly discontinuous with the processes already underway. The life Christians hope for is everlasting, not eternally fixed but always moving closer to perfection.

CONCLUSION

This chapter proposes that the ideals of truth, good, and beauty could advance the US culture to causes of universal significance and practical solidarity with the poor worldwide. The imitation of the God revealed by Jesus of Nazareth particularly in the realm of social and economic justice can ground a radiant hopefulness in the future that this God represents for all humanity. These ideals are not meant to be a panacea for the ills that afflict contemporary society, and none can be adequately achieved without profound ongoing conversion in all dimension of human life. However, these ideals can provide a vision of an ethical future that genuinely converted Christians can strive to achieve.

QUESTIONS FOR REFLECTION

1. Do you accept the premise that many members of the US culture are trapped in a system of false values from which they need to be liberated by sociopolitical and religious

conversion? Why or why not? If you agree with the premise, what concrete steps can you identify that could free people from this entrapment?

2. Compare Royce's concept of loyalty and John Paul II's notion of solidarity. Do you agree with the chapter's premise that they are equivalent? Why or why not?

3. Does Polanyi's alternative to free-market capitalism as presented here seem plausible to you? Why or why not? Do you think it is necessary to find ways to move beyond the ideology of the Liberal Creed? Why or why not? What are some practical steps that could alleviate the most negative aspects of free-market utopic ideology?

4. What qualities make a person worthy of imitation, in your view? Can you identify particular people that model authentic individual autonomy as described in this chapter? If so, how do they achieve this?

5. Do you agree with this chapter's assertion that most Americans have wishes rather than firm beliefs about the nature of life after death? Explain. If you are a religious adherent, how does your religion envision the future after death and how valid and compelling is this vision, in your view?

FOR FURTHER READING

Bellah, Robert, et al., *The Good Society* (New York: Alfred A. Knopf, 1991).

Bonhoeffer, Dietrich, *The Communion of Saints: A Dogmatic Inquiry into the Sociology of the Church*, trans., R. Gregor Smith (New York: Harper & Row, 1963).

Bynum, Caroline Walker, *The Resurrection of the Body in Western Christianity, 200–1336* (New York: Columbia University Press, 1995).

DuBois, W.E.B., *The Souls of Back Folks* (New York: Bantam Classic Edition, 1989).

Ellacuria, Ignacia, S.J., and Jon Sobrino SJ, eds., *Mysterium Liberationis: Fundamental Concepts of Liberation Theology* (Maryknoll, NY: Orbis Books, 1993).

Garcia-Rivera, Alejandro, *The Community of the Beautiful: A Theological Aesthetics* (Collegeville, MN: Liturgical Press, 1999).

————. *The Garden of God: A Theological Cosmology* (Minneapolis, MN: Fortress Press, 2009).

John Paul II, *On Social Concerns: Sollicitudo rei socialis* (Washington, DC: USCCB Publishing, 1988).

————. *On Human Work: Laborem exercens* (New York: Pauline Books & Media, 1981).

McDannell, Colleen, and Bernhard Lang, *Heaven: A History* (New Haven: Yale University Press, 1988).

Murphy-O'Connor, Jerome, *Becoming Human Together: The Pastoral Anthropology of St. Paul* (Wilmington, DE: Michael Glazier Press, 1982).

Polkinghorne, John, *The God of Hope and the End of the World* (New Haven: Yale University Press, 2002).

————. *Surprised by Hope: Rethinking Heaven, the Resurrection, and the Mission of the Church* (New York: Harper Collins, 2008).

Royce, Josiah, "The Philosophy of Loyalty," in *The Basic Writings of Josiah Royce*, ed. with introduction by John J. McDermott (Chicago: University of Chicago Press, 1969), 2:855–1013.

————. *The Problem of Christianity*, with introduction by John E. Smith (Chicago: University of Chicago Press, 1968).

Integral Adult Conversion and Christian Spirituality
Three Case Studies

> For all who are led by the Spirit of God are children of God. For you did not receive a spirit of slavery to fall back into fear, but you have received a spirit of adoption. When we cry, "Abba! Father!" it is that very Spirit bearing witness with our spirit that we are children of God, and if children, then heirs, heirs of God and joint heirs with Christ—if, in fact, we suffer with him so that we may also be glorified with him.
>
> — ROMANS 8:14–17

CHRISTIAN SPIRITUALITY AS FUNDAMENTALLY COMMUNAL

In America today, it's common to hear people say, "I'm not religious, but I am spiritual." Recent studies have shown that approximately 20 percent of Americans would describe themselves in this way.[1] This study also indicates, however, that the words *spiritual* and *religious* are synonyms. Both connote belief in a higher power of some kind. Both also imply a desire to connect, or enter into a more intense

---

1. See Robert Fuller, "Spiritual but Not Religious," at *www.beliefnet.com/Entertainment/ Books/2002/07/Spiritual-But-Not-Religious.aspx*.

relationship, with this higher power. Finally, both connote interest in rituals, practices, and moral behaviors that foster such a connection or relationship.[2] Nevertheless, in the public mind, they have come to have different meanings: spirituality resides in the private realm of experience, while religion concerns the public life of membership in religious institutions. The fact that they have become separated in the public's mind indicates that religious institutions are increasingly perceived as somehow nonspiritual or even anti-spiritual. How, then, can they function as communities that foster religious conversion, in the sense discussed earlier? What might they need to do to recapture their spiritual" identity?

TRINITARIAN SPIRITUALITY AND CHRISTIAN CONVERSION

In Christian theology, the Trinity is a single dynamic reality composed of distinct persons—God as a divine community. When believers allow the Spirit to transform them through religious conversion into the image of Christ, they come to participate in the divine community, and they also imitate this community in the human communities of which they are members. The Christian Trinitarian spirituality is a movement of the human spirit in relation to God and Jesus Christ in tandem with the promptings of the Holy Spirit. The Trinitarian spirituality is also a communal spirituality, with participation at both divine and human levels. Christianity is always relational. In Christian spirituality, the way that humans exist in God makes a difference to God, and the way that humans exist in God makes a difference to the way that God exists in each person.[3]

The starting point of Christian spirituality is always conversion: the acceptance of personal transformation and the ongoing dialogue with and in the Spirit of God. This process is simultaneously personal and communal. To be converted at the personal level and not be converted or participate in a converted community is to endanger or even subvert the personal conversion. Trinitarian

2. Ibid.

3. See Donald Gelpi, *The Divine Mother: A Trinitarian Theology of the Holy Spirit* (Lanham, MD: University Press of America, 1984), 83–101.

spirituality can never be an individualistic, self-centered quest, neither can it be a formalized and objective program without genuinely personal dimensions.

A great variety of "spiritualities" have developed throughout the Christian tradition. These spiritualties represent authentic schools, or particular patterns, of conversion. They may have different practices or symbols, different cultural or historical situations, even different philosophical foundations, but they all concern the whole person, they are all ongoing, and they are all communal as well as individual. Most types of Christian spirituality are based on the values of radical discipleship and community, not in place of personal growth and authenticity but as the conditions for the possibility of such fulfillment. As such, many traditional forms of spirituality offer the very thing that the culture needs: an integrated and coherent alternative vision that takes seriously cultural values without being subsumed by them. Inculturating spirituality in the North American context, therefore, is as much a process of recovery as adaptation.

THREE PERSONAL STORIES OF INTEGRAL ADULT CONVERSION AND CONTEMPORARY CHRISTIAN SPIRITUALITY

This chapter presents the conversion stories of three individuals known to the author. Each story tells of a process of integral, meaning whole or complete, conversion that was mediated by a Christian spiritual movement. They all found companions for their journey, who connected them to a more extensive process of holistic transformation than they could have found on their own. The stories all recount how the individuals were challenged to move beyond religious conversion to other forms of conversion by their participation in the life of a community. Particularly, all were enabled to engage the sociopolitical aspect of conversion in ways that went beyond the scope of charitable concern and moral kindness. Furthermore, each of these stories can function as a case study of the three wall-dismantling strategies outlined in the previous chapter. These stories attempt to tease out the nature of cultivating authentic individual autonomy, succeeding by imitating Christ, and developing hopefulness instead of superficial optimism. In each case, the person discovered that his or her faith required taking sociopolitical conversion seriously and greatly expanding the scope of the journey to include the social, political, and economic activity that each would have otherwise never known or considered. In the Christian tradition, holistic conversion demands that one move beyond personal growth and development to ultimately engage the world and its problems through direct action. Christian conversion leads believers to see past the walls of comfort and security so as to enter the universal struggle for justice, peace, and respect for human dignity.

Alex

Alex worked for many years in a local business started by his father and grandfather. Alex had branched out from their remarkable achievements and became a successful entrepreneur and local leader in his own right. While raised in a Catholic environment, Alex's interest in religion and philanthropy would not emerge until he was married with children of his own. By his own admission, his initial religious conversion began with an ACTS retreat he attended at the behest of his father, with whom he had a strained relationship, in the mid-1990s.

The ACTS Movement began in the 1980s in San Antonio, Texas, as an updated version of the Cursillo Movement. Both movements were understood to be short courses (*cursillo* literally means "short course" in Spanish) on the Catholic faith to revive and renew the spiritual lives of lay Catholics.[4] The ACTS Movement, based in the theology of Vatican II, tries to broaden its scope and access to include non-Catholics as well as Catholics who had stopped practicing. The ACTS Movement focused on four pillars: adoration, community, theology, and service. The movement shaped weekend retreats that combined personal faith sharing with traditional Christian symbols, rituals, and liturgical services as a means of enabling the ongoing conversion of both the retreatants and those giving the retreats. In South Texas alone, this movement has touched the lives of more than 350,000 men and women in the last twenty years.

---

4. See further *www.actsmission.org*.

Alex believes that his decision to attend his first ACTS retreat also marked the beginning of his affective conversion in that it worked to strengthen the relationship between Alex and his father and helped him to realize that he had to take personal responsibility for his own happiness and forgive the shortcomings of his father as a first step in a process of becoming a better father himself. The retreat awakened a spiritual hunger in Alex that he had not previously known and forged new bonds of understanding and respect between him and his father. Alex decided to become a member of an ACTS team to share his experience of enlightenment and renewed faith with others.

Over the next four or five years, Alex's involvement in the ACTS ministry intensified, and he found himself at the center of an emerging diocesan and eventually national movement dedicated to enabling spiritual awakening and revitalization for Catholic parishes and dioceses. In this movement, Alex also discovered a deep sense of community and shared purpose with an ever-widening circle of men who were outside his normal socioeconomic sphere. Alex found himself in a communion of "brothers" from every conceivable walk of life and level of personal and professional achievement. The boundaries of personal interaction that normally defined life in San Antonio seemed not to inhibit the members of this community. This growing community of spiritual communion and personal friendship encouraged Alex to turn his considerable intellectual gifts to a critical reflection on the movement and its theological foundations. Alex decided to pursue a graduate degree from an area Catholic school of theology and ministry.

Alex found that he was successful at academic studies and found them personally and intellectually invigorating. At the same time, members of the academic community in which Alex was enrolled found his powerful skills in business and organization to offer a significantly new insight into the areas of theological investigation. His professors also realized that Alex's organizational acumen offered an invaluable asset to the church. Alex's ecclesial and pastoral identity began to emerge out of this process. He began to realize that he was being called to both a personal and professional life of service to the church as a teacher, spiritual guide, and pastoral leader. At this point, Alex decided to dedicate himself full time to a graduate education in philosophy and theology and ministerial activity in the ACTS Movement.

Through this process of acute engagement with fellow scholars and spiritual companions in ministry, Alex began to feel a call to a deeper commitment to sociopolitical causes. Through friends and previous experience in business, he found himself becoming more deeply involved in the local Catholic Worker house, which was dedicated to providing hospitality and relief to homeless men and women. During the previous five years, the members of the community supporting this Catholic Worker house found themselves caught between the citywide effort to address the problem of homelessness and its causes and the increasing political and economic pressure on the local government to make the inner city welcoming to the tourist industry that acts as one of the largest sources of wealth for the city.

Alex was elected as president of the board of the Catholic Worker house at a time when it found itself in direct conflict with the city and neighborhood residents over its practice of offering hospitality and services to the homeless. The city had designated a single new facility as the sole provider of services to the local indigent and homeless population and wanted all other charities to cease their services and direct those in need to the single provider. Unfortunately, this institution was not large enough to provide for all those who needed services, neither was it willing to assist all of those who were homeless and in need. There exists a certain percentage of homeless men and women who simply cannot fulfill the requirements of the citywide facility and were, therefore, being denied some of the most basic services that humans require. The supporters of the Catholic Worker house decided that it still needed to provide a place for these men and women to go during the day and to offer them some basic services they needed.

Alex found himself at the center of a controversy that often pitted him against the very city and civic leaders that he counted as friends and allies during his business career. These friends were disillusioned with Alex and even embarrassed or angry at his public defense of the poor and homeless. Alex increasingly advocated for a sociopolitical cause that put him in direct conflict with both people and principles that he previously held dear. At the same time, his collaborators at the Catholic Worker house were impressed by his strong organizational and advocacy skills now at the service of their cause. Alex was beginning to realize as well that what began as a charitable project had increasingly become an issue of basic justice deeply important to him. He had become friends with many homeless people and no longer saw them as mere objects of his pity. Alex had entered into a relationship of solidarity with the members of the Catholic Worker community and identified the plight of the homeless as his own. Furthermore, Alex realized that the particular injustice faced by the homeless in San Antonio was inherently tied to a much wider web of injustice with deep social, political, economic, and spiritual roots in the very American society that has afforded him so much opportunity. Alex now sees that any particular struggle for justice cannot be severed from a broader search for the new heaven and the new earth promised by Jesus Christ in the gospel.

Bryan

Bryan was born in a small northeastern town, the son of a prominent family that was part of a small-town Catholic culture that he found comforting. He felt nurtured and valued in his local church and developed a lifelong relationship with one particularly wise and supportive pastor. After he left for college and developed a successful career as a small businessman, he found that the Catholic Church's attitude toward his sexual orientation made his ongoing participation difficult. He eventually found a home in the Episcopal Church. There he found a church community that not only supported him but also challenged him to move beyond his personal sphere of comfort in charitable endeavors. Through his church he became deeply involved in service at the local homeless shelter and in fundraising for efforts to feed and clothe the less fortunate. Together with his life partner, Bryan's business prospered and his social life flourished.

Ten years ago Bryan found himself inexplicably depressed and suffering the effects of physical illnesses that left him practically debilitated. He had found that his personal life had grown increasingly painful and that his professional life was no longer fruitful or satisfying. Through the efforts of his partner and some close friends,

Bryan came to realize that he was struggling with addiction and needed a serious intervention and fundamental change of lifestyle. As Bryan began to move away from the actual addiction and work through his twelve-step program, he began to realize that the source of his addiction was actually a deeper need for meaning and spiritual enlightenment. Bryan discovered that he not only missed the religious comfort of his childhood but also felt that he was being called to some deeper form of interpretation and integration of prayer and spirituality in his life.

Through a series of coincidences, Bryan was invited to attend a weekend retreat on mediation under the directed by Father Thomas Keating. During this retreat, Bryan learned a contemplation technique called Centering Prayer. In this, he discovered a method of personal prayer and an approach to the whole of his life that was transformative. Over time, Bryan became involved in the spirituality and justice outreach arm of the Centering Prayer movement called Contemplative Outreach. Contemplative Outreach began in the 1980s with the pioneering work of Keating and the monks at St. Joseph Abbey in Spencer, Massachusetts.[5] This program encouraged him to integrate centering prayer into his twelve-step program and to see prayer and meditation as a springboard to direct social and political activism on behalf of justice for the oppressed.

Five years ago, Bryan accepted an invitation by a colleague in the Centering Prayer movement to visit the county jail and consider substitute-teaching a class for him at the jail. Bryan was extremely hesitant about even going to the county jail, let alone teaching inmates. Through his practice of centering prayer, however, he was able to perceive a call to accept this invitation and to trust that it would manifest a deeper invitation in his life. Bryan has been working as a part-time volunteer chaplain at the jail ever since. He teaches a class on centering prayer twice a week and teaches in a program designed to bring together centering-prayer techniques with traditional twelve-step programs as a way of enriching the spiritual dimension of the twelve-step programs for the inmates. Bryan also visits and counsels individual prisoners and works with

---

5. See *www.contemplativeoutreach.org/history-contemplative-outreach*.

a team of volunteer chaplains, coordinated by two religious sisters, who serve as the only paid chaplains for the facility. This team of chaplains provides the sole spiritual and religious services to the jail, a facility that houses more than four thousand prisoners in various stages of the judicial system.

Bryan's experience at the jail has awakened him to the deep level of confusion and self-deception at the heart of the human experience. He claims that practically every prisoner he speaks to asks him the same question: "How did I get here? How did I become the type of person that ends up in prison?" Bryan has come to realize how often we as humans are unconscious of our deepest motivations and driven by vices and addictions that shape us in ways that go completely contrary to our own plans and desires. Bryan believes that centering prayer offers a means of empowering people to critically access their lives and to make conscious choices that enable them to act in ways that are consistent with their better self. Bryan hopes that through his work he is able to penetrate the hidden walls of denigration and self-loathing that often drive good people into self-destructive patterns of behavior. He believes that his personal transformation and enlightenment were actually an opportunity or call to devote his life to the most marginalized and literally outcast members of his community.

Bryan claims the last five years have formed in him a deep well of empathy that has moved him beyond simple pity for those he works with and afforded him the ability to identify with them and their plight. He has come to see that in reality he has much more in common with those he ministers to than with members of the class and social system that he comes from. Moreover, through his collaboration with a community of religious women who minister at the jail, Bryan has entered into a Christian community that has affected him at every level of his life. This community has given him a sense of solidarity with the poor that he was unaware of previously. It has also united him with a group of women and men who share his passion for service and justice that emerges out of their shared prayer and spiritual journey. He feels like this community of prayer and service is not only supporting and empowering him for ministry but also is challenging him to move into deeper levels of sociopolitical conversion.

Nancy

Nancy was born in a small midwestern city and raised in a loving and nurturing Catholic family that put great emphasis on the practice of their faith. She attended Catholic parochial schools and a small Catholic university at which she prepared to be a secondary school teacher. After college, she taught for two years in the Teach for America program, which placed her in a very troubled inner-city school in New Orleans, Louisiana, teaching social studies to seventh graders. Overall, she found the experience traumatizing and depressing: Nancy found her efforts at teaching faltering and the whole school system to be deeply flawed and counterproductive. She lost confidence in her own ability as a teacher and developed a deep anxiety about the future of American culture and plight of the "other America" as she described it. The only really positive development during these two years was that she met and fell in love with her future husband.

After Nancy and Kevin married, they moved to the suburban enclave of a major US city so that he could pursue a job as an accountant in a major firm. They settled into a middle-class lifestyle having three children in the next five years and becoming active in their local Catholic parish and eventually in its school and children's activities. Nancy remained unsettled and unresolved about her teaching experience. Though she decided not to work so that she could stay home to raise their children, she became very involved with an early-childhood program for children with special needs and learning deficits. Nancy also became devoted to the right-to-life movement and worked with her local parish and other groups to protest abortion providers in her area.

During this time she met a woman who invited her to deepen her faith and spirituality through a Catholic lay movement called the Focolare Movement, founded by Chiara Lubich with a group of companions during World War II in Italy. The word *focolare* in Italian means "hearth" or "fireside." The movement's goal is to build a community of love centered on the word of God that would provide a home and a source of guidance for lay people.[6] The Focolare Movement finds its

---

6. See further *www.focolare.us/us/spirituality*.

deepest foundation in the prayer of Jesus "that they may all be one" (Jn 17:21). This prayer animates all of the actions of the movement toward unity within the Christian church and between people of different religious traditions.

In the Focolare Movement, Nancy discovered the kind of spirituality that nurtured her strong faith and identity as a wife and mother and challenged her to move beyond her comfort zone to reach out to all kinds of people in unity and solidarity. The movement also helped her to integrate her spiritual and ecclesial life with all the aspects of daily experience and to see in each moment an opportunity to make Christ present. As she became more deeply involved in the organization of the movement in her area, she was also able to recover some of the teaching skills that had played such an important part in her early identity. She not only became a speaker at conferences and retreats in the movement but also understood that her ability to share that her experience of finding Christ in daily life enabled others to expand their own conscious experiences of unity.

During this time, Nancy continued to devote herself to anti-abortion political movements but chose to find unity and compassionate engagement with the many young women that she encountered who were seeking abortions or at least considering this option. She also chose not to see the members of the Planned Parenthood clinic where she organized as evil or horrible people, realizing that Christ was present among them as well. This openness to finding oneness even with the people she opposed manifested itself when she realized that a woman from her neighborhood—their children attended the same school—was employed as a counselor at the Planned Parenthood clinic. Instead of confronting or simply ignoring her, Nancy decided that she needed to try to find a source of unity with this woman. This has led to a long and unlikely cooperation and even friendship between these two women. They developed a shared effort to support these young women through pregnancy and help them decide whether to parent or make adoption plans. They also developed strategies to make parenting viable for those mothers choosing not to make adoption plans. Over time, Nancy was able to see that this other woman was a devout Christian devoted to helping young women choose to improve their lives and those of their children. She actually found an ally in this woman who similarly found an ally in her. Nancy became a source of encouragement and resource to many young women that her friend identified. She would simply accompany them to doctor's visits, listen to their problems; help them find jobs or clothes or transportation during and after their pregnancies. Nancy became the kind of ongoing companion that no state agency or social service could ever provide to these young pregnant women. Nancy's friend found that she could reliably refer young women to her, knowing that she would neither judge nor proselytize them but would respect their hard choices and the complex assortment of issues that made up their lives.

Nancy also found herself drawn into the role of advocate for these women as well as an increasingly vocal advocate for better local and state services for women in all stages of life. Without diminishing her antiabortion stance, she realized that her pro-life political activities needed to include organizing for an array of health, education, and social services that often went contrary to the political views of her normal political allies. Nancy found herself simultaneously on both ends of the political spectrum in a way that often confused her colleagues, family, husband, and pastor. She found that the members of the Focolare Movement often supported her desire for unity and her commitment to social justice even if they did not always understand exactly how her political affiliations converged with her religious commitments.

Nancy became a well-known advocate for a variety of political causes and began to see her vocation to be a teacher in a new light. She realized that she needed to teach people on all sides of the political spectrum about the demands of justice and the wider implications of promoting life and human dignity. She also realized that she was called to develop relationships of shared advocacy across denominational and religious lines in a way that promoted a greater unity between all kinds of people who desired justice and life-promoting political action. As a speaker, writer, and now blogger, Nancy has been able to bring a widely diverse contingent of well-intentioned people into a civil dialogue about the most effective ways to work together to achieve projects they share in common and to listen to and even support each other when they disagree about policy and practical political ends.

CONCLUSION

"By faith Moses . . . refused to be called a son of Pharaoh's daughter, choosing rather to share ill-treatment with the people of God than to enjoy the fleeting pleasures of sin. He considered abuse . . . to be greater wealth than the treasures of Egypt, for he was looking ahead to the reward" (Heb 11:24–26). Conversion evokes a fundamental reorientation of the life of the converted. It changes not just how one views the world but also how one acts or reacts to the concrete events of life. In the biblical account, Moses' sense of empathy and solidarity with the Hebrew people changed his life and the life of the community that he came to embrace. His faith enlivened the faith of people unsure that their God still heard and cared for them. God delivered the Hebrew people out of their seeming invisibility to the Promised Land. Moses put his faith and hope in God and was able, over time, to convey that same faith and hope to the Hebrew people in a way that empowered and freed them. Faith, hope, and love are not merely feelings or emotions people have: they, like forces of nature, change and shape history as dramatically as either physical forces or false value systems.

The figure of Moses serves as a reminder that liberation depends on conversion and that conversion depends on the ability to see the world from another point of view than the conventional wisdom that societies normally afford their members. The story of Moses also signals that those enmeshed in the structures of wealth and power need to be liberated from false values and misguided loyalties that keep them from seeing the world the way that God sees it and intends it to be. Authentic conversion gives one new eyes and new ears to envision an alternative reality and a different destiny than the closed sense of comfort, security, and complacency that life in the first world normally allows. Genuine Christian conversion is one way people can become free. Christians learn to believe that God is love and loves everyone. They understand themselves as called to love others unconditionally through practical solidarity with the poor, oppressed, and outcast of this world and to hope that there is an ultimate reward for such a life.

Holistic spirituality necessarily implies integral adult conversion. Though encompassing many different traditions and models of religious experience, the goal of the Christian spiritual life is to integrate God's grace with human nature analogously to the Incarnation of Jesus Christ. This means that Christian spirituality will never be just about religion or interior spiritual enlightenment—although it includes these experiences—but ultimately requires that people integrate their religious experience with all the other areas of human experience, including the sociopolitical dimension of their lives. The great traditions of spirituality, as well as new emerging modes of shared spiritual life, serve to guide individuals in their personal attempts to integrate the spiritual with the natural dimensions of their life, and the personal with the communal. Viewed from the perspective of Christian theology, the Spirit of God guides all those who experience it in a process of integrating the divine life into their own lives and cooperating with this divine life in bringing the reign of God into the sociopolitical, cultural, and economic aspects of human history.

QUESTIONS FOR REFLECTION

1. Do you believe that spirituality should encourage community? Do you think that it is fundamentally communal? Explain.

2. If you are part of a spiritual tradition, what part of that tradition most encourages communal and social dimensions of religious experience? How does your spiritual tradition require and enable sociopolitical conversion?

3. Do you know people that represent the kind of integral adult conversion advocated in this text? What is their story? Can you identify with any of the stories presented here? Why or why not?

4. Consider each of the chapter's personal stories in light of the three wall-dismantling strategies described in chapter 8. Identify elements in the stories that illustrate (a) the cultivation of individual autonomy, (b) success following from imitating Christ, and (c) the emergence of authentic hope and diminishment of superficial optimism.

5. What are the overall themes that run through all of the stories presented here? What are the critical elements of holistic conversion that are present in all of these stories?

6. Do you identify with the biblical figure of Moses? If so, do elements of his story lead to insights about your life? Explain.

FOR FURTHER READING AND STUDY

Au, Wilkie, *By Way of the Heart: Toward a Holistic Christian Spirituality* (Mahwah, NJ: Paulist Press, 1989).

Bonhoeffer, Dietrich, *The Cost of Discipleship* (New York: Touchstone, 1995).

Downey, Michael, *Understanding Christian Spirituality* (New York: Paulist Press, 1997).

Groody, Daniel G., *Globalization, Spirituality, and Justice* (Mayknoll, NY: Orbis Books, 2007).

Kees, Waaijman, *Spirituality: Forms, Foundations, Methods* (Leuven: Peeters, 2002).

Nouwen, Henri, *The Way of the Heart* (New York: Seabury, 1981).

Rolheiser, Ronald, *The Holy Longing: The Search for Christian Spirituality* (New York: Doubleday, 1999).

——. *The Shattered Lantern: Rediscovering a Felt Presence of God* (New York: Crossroads, 2005).

Sheldrake, Philip, *Spirituality: A Brief History* (Oxford and Malden, MA: Wiley-Blackwell, 2013).

——. *Explorations in Spirituality: History, Theology and Social Practice* (New York: Paulist Press, 2010).

Teasdale, Wayne, *The Mystic Heart: Discovering a Universal Spirituality in the World's Religions* (Novato, CA: New World Library, 2001).

Index

A

"Abba," 94, 113–14, 173
Abel, 42
acceptance, 66–67
accountability, 22, 32, 85, 90. See
 also responsibility and obligation
actions (works)
 centering prayer and, 180, 181
 change and, 89
 conversion and, 176
 faith and, 11
 hope and, 66
 intellectual conversion and, 96
 private *versus* public, 91
 religious conversion and, 98
 sociopolitical conversion and, 93
 See also service; sociopolitical
  conversion
activism, 97
ACTS Movement, 176–77, 178
Acts of the Apostles (Luke), 67n6
Adam and Eve, 23, 42
addiction, 180, 181
adulation, 46
advertising, 55–56
aesthetics, 71, 73, 87, 156, 159–79,
 168
affective conversion, 86–88, 96, 97,
 139, 177
affective realm of experience, 83,
 84, 94

Afghanistan war, 63
African Americans, 73–74
afterlife (heaven), 163–68, 166n47
Albingensianism, 117
ambition, 45, 49, 54, 55, 154. See
 also success
American dream, 54–56, 57, 69,
 70–71, 74, 129, 130
American Enlightenment, 109–10
American philosophy, 82
Americans. See United States and
 North America
An American Tragedy (Dreiser),
 53–55, 56
Amish communities, 51, 56
Anabaptists, 51
Ananias, 80
anawim, 17
anti-abortion activity, 182, 183
antidepressants, 66
Aquinas, Thomas, 44–45, 45n3
Arab Americans, 26
Aristotle, 44, 44n1, 53
Arrupe, Pedro, 147
artists, 68–70
Asian Americans, 26
atheists, American, 108n15
atonement, 157–58, 157n29, 161,
 168–69
Augustine of Hippo, 106
Augustinians, 136